Sunday Morning Readers' Theater

---

19 Congregational
Worship Resources
Cycle A

Pamela Urfer

CSS Publishing Company, Inc.
Lima, Ohio

SUNDAY MORNING READERS' THEATER, A

Scripture quotations are from the *New Revised Standard Version of the Bible,* copyright 1989 by the Division of Christian Education of the National Council of the Churches of Christ in the USA. Used by permission.

Library of Congress Cataloging-in-Publication Data
(Revised for vol. 1)

Urfer, Pamela.
  Sunday morning readers' theater.

  Contents: [1] Cycle A — [2] Cycle B — [3] Cycle C.
  1. Drama in public worship. 2. Worship programs. 3. Christian drama, American. I. Title.
BV289.U74 1994   246.7   93-43354
  ISBN 0-7880-0569-3 (v. 1)
  ISBN 1-55673-518-9 (v. 2)
  ISBN 0-7880-0214-7 (v. 3)

ISBN: 0-7880-0569-3

Sunday Morning Readers' Theater A

Table Of Contents

Introduction

Readers' Theater is an old dramatic form which has found a new meaning in modern church settings. Many church drama groups are coming to prefer it to more traditional dramatics as it requires no memorization of lines, no sets, costumes, or blocking, and no special training. Yet Readers' Theater can be just as effective, dramatically, as the most polished traditional presentation.

Readers' Theater scripts are designed to be read aloud rather than recited. They are short and to the point, usually five to ten minutes long, and can be incorporated successfully into Sunday services. In this collection they are used as dramatic illustrations of the scripture readings of the day, but they could as easily be employed as a springboard for the sermon or the focus of a church celebration.

Preparation

All that's needed for a Readers' Theater presentation is the script, a stiff folder to put it in, and a stool for each participant. The actors sit in front of the congregation, holding their scripts, and read their lines clearly and loudly, either with or without the aid of a microphone.

It's best if the actors glance at their scripts only while the other actors are saying their parts then speak their own

7

lines looking directly out at the audience. This eliminates the problem of muttering into the page. It's the same principle a choir employs: though singers glance frequently at their music, they must sing out the words with chins up and eyes forward.

This use of scripts eliminates much of the anxiety associated with amateur dramatics as well as most of the tedium of rehearsals. Even so, the actors should take the time to read carefully through their scripts at home. They should feel confident that they know how to pronounce every word and are aware of what others around them will be doing.

At least one complete run-through should be held before the actual performance so the actors can familiarize themselves with timing and placement and practice gestures and facial expressions. In certain situations, actors may be required to memorize a few lines so that they have the freedom to move about the acting area. These occasions have been kept to a minimum and are usually presented as options.

Advantages Of Readers' Theater

It may seem awkward to restrict actors' movements to what can be accomplished while seated, but this method has one great advantage: since many churches lack a useful staging area, or are encumbered by immovable pulpits, pulpit platforms, or a fixed railing surround, traditional dramatic productions may be out of the question — there's simply no place for actors to go.

Readers' Theater, requiring only enough space for three or four stools, can fit in almost anywhere — at either side of the pulpit and on the same level, between pulpit and first row, or, if necessary, at the head of the center aisle. The director should check the sight lines from various parts of the sanctuary to discover the most advantageous position.

If the stools will not be in the way during the service, they might be put in place beforehand and left there until time for the skit. This has the advantage of heightening the interest of the audience. If the skit occurs early in the service, the stools can be taken off by the actors as they leave in order to free up space for the choir or speaker. If other activities are taking place in that area before it's time for the skit, the actors can bring the stools in with them as they enter.

Tall stools with rungs are best. They raise the actor a little above the level of the observers and the rungs provide a steadying influence. Generally, natural colored wood blends better with various time periods than plastic or metal. The stools should be lightweight enough for the actors to carry on and off stage themselves.

Acting Skills

At first, the director can encourage participation in the drama group by all who are interested. Later, she may wish to make decisions as to which actors work best in which parts. Beginners should not be made to feel they are too inexperienced to convey the emotions called for by the script. Many Readers' Theater skits have a comic element and over-acting is often appropriate. And for those who can't quite "let themselves go," even a subdued reading gets the idea across.

Moderate bodily actions and gestures can be used to emphasize the meaning of the spoken lines. This is where the actors' hidden talents can shine forth. Whether turning toward someone with a threatening stare or turning away to offer a cold shoulder, pretending to sip tea daintily from a cup or to stuff their mouth with pizza, the actors can let themselves go in their upper-body movements.

Facial expressions are also useful. They clue the audience as to the character's emotions, whether fright, distrust, anger or compassion. The use of costumes is optional, but they do give the audience a better idea of who's who and can provide the actor with an easier transition into his characterization.

Drama In The Church

The use of drama in a worship service constitutes a break with tradition in many churches and some in the congregation may feel uncomfortable. A few words of introduction by one of the staff — preferably the senior pastor — will help make Readers' Theater more acceptable. The pastor might like to add a short account of how even Jesus used parables and dramatic situations to get his point across.

With a little practice on the part of the drama group, Readers' Theater can provide as much opportunity for actual performing as any traditional dramatic presentation. With the pressure to memorize eliminated, directors may find that congregational members who had never before thought of themselves as "dramatic types" are eager to explore this new art. They will soon find themselves having great fun as they give glory to God and pleasure to their audience through drama.

Who's Coming?

Cast: NOAH, SHIBAH (his wife), 1ST NEIGHBOR (man), 2ND NEIGHBOR (older woman), 3RD NEIGHBOR (younger woman)

Length: 7 minutes

NOAH and SHIBAH are seated on stools, center stage. There is an empty stool next to SHIBAH.

SHIBAH: Well, husband. It seems the ark building is coming along nicely.

NOAH: Yes. We should be ready for the rain in three or four days.

SHIBAH: *(Looking at the sky)* It won't be too long now, clouds are starting to form. I do hope the Lord God will change his mind and hold back the flood.

NOAH: Why would he do that?

SHIBAH: Why? Because of all the people that will die — mothers, fathers, little children. It will be a terrible disaster, the worst the world has ever known.

NOAH: But these are bad people. They deserve to die.

SHIBAH: How do you know that?

NOAH: Because the Lord God said so. Don't you believe him?

SHIBAH: I don't know. They can't all be bad, can they?

NOAH: *(Shrugs)* Who knows? Why don't you ask them yourself?

SHIBAH: Fine! I will. The next time one of the townspeople comes to ask what we're doing, I'll see if I can find out.

The 1ST NEIGHBOR enters and takes the stool next to SHIBAH.

1ST: Howdy, Shibah, Noah. Looks like your ark is almost finished.

NOAH: Yes, it is. We're going to be leaving soon. Would you like to join us?

1ST: *(Laughs)* You've asked me that every day for a year. No, I don't think so.

SHIBAH: Things are going to get pretty bad around here.

1ST: You religious types are always saying that. Gloom and doom. That's all it ever is with you.

SHIBAH: *(Thoughtfully)* You don't seem like a bad person.

1ST: *(Huffily)* Of course I'm not a bad person. I'm a pretty good person, if I do say so myself.

SHIBAH: Then why is God leaving you behind?

1ST: God isn't leaving me behind; I'm choosing to stay. Even if what you say is true, that there's a great flood coming — which I don't believe for a minute — I'm not sure I would care to be saved. What kind of a world would there be when it was all over? What kind of a world would it be, ruled by a god who is willing to massacre thousands of innocent people?

SHIBAH: That *is* a puzzle.

NOAH: I'll tell you what kind of a world it will be. It will be a clean world, a pure world, with all the riff-raff and wickedness swept away.

1ST: *(Angrily)* Are you referring to me, sir?

NOAH: Not necessarily. There's plenty of wickedness out there without counting you.

1ST: You're right. I'm a good person, but there are lots in the town who aren't. Well, I must be going. I'm having a party at my house next week and I have to meet with the caterers. I'd invite you but you probably won't be here.

NOAH: No, we probably won't.

1ST: Well, see you around.

He leaves.

SHIBAH: Well, there's one good person at least. I don't know what God can be thinking of to kill him off.

NOAH: I think he's lying.

SHIBAH: Who? God?

NOAH: No, our neighbor. We have only his word for it that he's a good person.

SHIBAH: Well, let's see about this one. She doesn't look very evil.

2ND NEIGHBOR enters and takes the stool by SHIBAH.

2ND: Hi, Shibah, Noah. Still working on that crazy boat project, I see.

SHIBAH: Yes, we are. Wouldn't you like to come with us?

2ND: No, I don't like God's plan, if that's what it really is. I've heard what he's said about us, or rather, what you say he's said, and I don't think it's very nice. He told us to mend our wicked ways — or else. Well, I, for one, have no wicked ways.

NOAH: No?

2ND: Absolutely not! And I don't like his insinuations that I have. God is entirely too fussy if he thinks the little mistakes I make are anything like wickedness. There's a lot of wickedness going on around here, I'll admit, but it doesn't have anything to do with me.

NOAH: Are you sure you wouldn't like to leave it all behind and make a new start with God's help?

2ND: There's nothing wrong with the world the way it is. It's never going to be perfect, if that's what you're looking for. Well, I'd better get on my way. My daughter's getting married next month and I have a million things to do.

She leaves.

SHIBAH: Now, you can't say *she's* evil. She's just trying to make the best of things.

NOAH: I'm not the one who says these people are evil. I'm just taking God's word for it. But it does make me suspicious that they all put the blame on someone else.

SHIBAH: Yes, it does seem funny that no one has done *anything* wrong.

3RD NEIGHBOR enters and takes the stool.

3RD: Hi, Shibah, Noah. Are you still convinced God is telling you to build this ark to escape from the disaster that's coming?

NOAH: Yes.

3RD: Would you mind if I came along?

SHIBAH: What?

3RD: I've been thinking about what you said, about how we've gotten so far away from God's will and fallen into wickedness, and I agree.

NOAH: I know: There's a lot of it around but it doesn't have anything to do with you.

3RD: No, it has everything to do with me. I've done my bit to make this world a miserable place to live and I'm sorry. I'd like to do better but it's hard in this environment. Perhaps if I were to get away and be by myself, or with friends, for a while, I'd get myself straight.

SHIBAH: Well, you're lucky. We just happen to have one opening left.

NOAH: We do?

SHIBAH: You know God said we could take a wife for each of the boys and Japeth hasn't found one yet. *(To 3RD NEIGHBOR)* If you wouldn't mind?

3RD: No, Japeth's always been a good friend. Great! I'll go grab a few things.

She leaves.

NOAH: So you finally found one who isn't evil.

SHIBAH: I didn't find her, she found us. Or, rather, she knows she needs God's help — and ours — to make things right in her life.

NOAH: Maybe that's what God was talking about all along. Maybe true wickedness isn't all the bad things we do, or lack of purity, but just not seeing our need for God.

SHIBAH: You're right. But it's hard. At least it is for me. I need God's help to trust him when it looks as if he's doing something unfair and hurtful.

NOAH: I know what you mean. Wickedness isn't as easy to define as I'd like it to be. Well, come on. We still have to load the last of the animal food.

SHIBAH: I hope that girl makes it back in time.

NOAH: And I hope Japeth appreciates what we've done.

SHIBAH: Amen!

They leave, arm in arm.

Sibling Rivalry

Cast: NARRATOR, MINISTER

Length: 8 minutes

There are two empty stools located in the center of the acting area. The officiating MINISTER announces the skit and takes a seat in the audience. The NARRATOR takes the pulpit or some other commanding position and begins to read.

NARR: "A man planted a vineyard and leased it to tenants and went to another country for a long time. When the season came, he sent a slave to the tenants in order that they might give him his share of the produce of the vineyard. But the tenants beat him and sent him away empty-handed. Next he sent another slave; that one also they beat and insulted and sent away empty-handed."

MIN: *(From his seat)* Ahem! Excuse me!

NARR: *(Ignoring him)* "And he sent still a third. This one also they wounded and threw out."

MIN: *(Standing)* Pardon me! May I ask —?

NARR: *(Ignoring him)* "Then the owner of the vineyard said, 'What shall I do? I will send my beloved son. Perhaps they will respect him.' "

MIN: *(Louder)* Excuse me! I believe you are reading the wrong scripture. That's the Parable of the Wicked Tenants. Our reading today is from Romans.

NARR: No, no. It's all right. Really.

MIN: But ...!

NARR: No, it will all work out. You'll see. Trust me.

MIN: *(Reluctantly)* Well, if you say so.

The MINISTER takes his seat.

NARR: "The son of the owner of the vineyard also had two sons. The elder one said to his father, 'Father, give me the share of the inheritance that will belong to me.' "

MIN: *(From his seat)* Er, pardon me.

The NARRATOR glances nervously at the MINISTER but goes ahead.

NARR: "So he divided his inheritance between them. The elder one took his inheritance and travelled to a distant country while the younger one stayed home and was a good and obedient son to his father."

MIN: *(Standing)* Excuse me! But you've still got the wrong reading. Today's reading is from Romans and it's about the Jews and the Gentiles. You're telling us the Parable of the Prodigal Son. And even then you're getting it all wrong. It's the *younger* son who —

NARR: No, no. It's okay. Really. Trust me.

MIN: *(Walking into the acting area)* I'm afraid I can't do that. You're making a complete mess of things. *(Shaking his head, to the AUDIENCE)* I always knew it was a mistake to include drama in the Sunday morning service.

NARR: *(Anxiously)* No. Please don't cancel the skit. I can make it better. Really I can! Let's sit down like reasonable people and talk this over.

MIN: I don't see what good that will do. *(Reluctantly)* But, all right. Just for a moment.

The NARRATOR and the MINISTER take the two stools in the center of the acting area.

MIN: Now what's happening here? Why can't you give us a skit based on today's reading? Is that so hard?

NARR: But I am! You just didn't let me finish.

MIN: Well, all right then. Go ahead. But be careful!

NARR: Thanks. Okay. *(Reads)* "So the father of the two sons went back to his own father, the owner of the vineyard, to ask him what to do. And he said, 'The greatest must become like the youngest and the leader like the one who serves. Who is greater: the one who is at table or the one who serves?' "

MIN: Hey! Wait a minute!

NARR: *(Ignoring him)* "So the father sent a message to his eldest son saying, 'I am among you as the one who serves.' "

MIN: Stop this right now!

NARR: *(Innocently)* Why? What's the matter?

19

MIN: You know very well what's the matter. This has nothing to do with today's reading. And, besides, you're mixing everything up.

NARR: You're right. I am. But that was the only thing I could think of to do. There's no parable based on the problem between the Gentiles and the Jews.

MIN: What problem? There's no problem between the Gentiles and the Jews.

NARR: No?

MIN: *(After a moment)* Well, yes. Maybe there is. But I don't see how your mixed-up parable is going to help that.

NARR: If you would just give me a chance I could show you. *(Wheedling)* Just a little chance? *(Holding up fingers an inch apart)* Just a teeny-weeny chance?

MIN: *(Irritated)* Oh, all right! But it had better be good.

NARR: It is. Trust me!

The MINISTER rolls his eyes.

NARR: Okay! Here we go! *(Reading)* "So the father ..." *(To the MINISTER)* That's the second father, the father of the two sons ...

MIN: Yes, I've got that.

NARR: "The father told his eldest son, 'I come to you, the circumcised, as a servant on behalf of the truth of God in order that I might confirm the promises given to the patriarchs.' "

20

MIN: Well, at least now we're back to today's reading.

NARR: "But the eldest son didn't pay any attention. He took his inheritance and went away. When he had spent everything, a severe famine took place throughout the country and he began to be in great need."

MIN: Serves him right.

The NARRATOR gives him a funny look but continues the reading.

NARR: Meanwhile, back at the ranch ...

The MINISTER gives him a hard look. The NARRATOR looks embarrassed, but goes on.

NARR: *(Reading)* "... the younger son has been listening to his father's every word and doing everything he was supposed to and behaving in a totally admirable way."

MIN: As he should.

NARR: "Still, the father was pining away for his eldest. So one day he tells his younger son, 'My heart is breaking for my lost son. I think I will go and look for him.' "

MIN: Now, this isn't —

The NARRATOR looks worried. The MINISTER sighs in resignation.

MIN: Oh, go ahead!

NARR: "The younger son, the good son says, 'But, Father! that isn't fair! I've been such a good son to you and my brother has caused you nothing but grief. Why do you even bother? You should punish him for what he has done instead of running off to look for him. And you should reward me for staying here and helping and being a good boy when I would have enjoyed a little running off with the money myself.' The father said, 'Yes, you have been a good boy and I do appreciate it. But my eldest is special to me. He is the apple of my eye. He and I go way back, back before you were ever born.' When the younger son seemed unconvinced, the father said, 'Who do you know that has a hundred sheep and losing one of them, does not leave the ninety-nine in the wilderness and go after the one who is lost?' "

The MINISTER again rolls his eyes.

NARR: "Still the youngest son didn't understand, so his father said, 'You have benefitted so much from all your brother did before you arrived. It is because of him that you are heir to this great ranch you see before you. It is because of him that you now have hope that your life may mean something. I have become your brother's servant so that he might someday be convinced to return home. If that were to happen, you will find yourself glorifying God for his mercy to your older brother.' But the younger son said, 'I hate my brother! I hate him for taking his inheritance and squandering it and I hate him for the pain he has caused you. Whatever grief I can cause him in this world, I will, for he doesn't deserve any better.' The father said, 'It makes me sad to hear that. I had hoped that you would welcome one another, just as I have welcomed both of you, for the glory of God.' "

MIN: Well, I must admit that is a very interesting parable. How does it end?

NARR: *(Gathering up her papers)* There isn't any ending. Not yet.

MIN: But you can't just leave it like that!

NARR: It isn't up to me. Not completely. As today's reading says, *(To the AUDIENCE)* "Welcome one another, therefore just as Christ has welcomed you, for the glory of God."

The NARRATOR leaves and the MINISTER, shaking his head in consternation, resumes his duties.

Taking Offense

Cast: JESUS, 1ST JOHN'S DISCIPLE, 2ND JOHN'S DIS-CIPLE, 1ST FOLLOWER, 2ND FOLLOWER (Gender is not important among the DISCIPLES and FOLLOWERS)

Length: 9 minutes

JESUS is seated on the center stool of three with his eyes down-cast, as if he were praying. Two FOLLOWERS stand a respect-ful distance behind him but still close enough to hear his words. JOHN'S DISCIPLES enter and take the stools on either side of him.

JESUS: Good morning.

1ST JOHN: Good morning, Master. May we talk with you?

JESUS: Certainly!

2ND JOHN: We are two of John's disciples.

JESUS: How is he?

1ST JOHN: We have just come from visiting him in prison. He is as well as can be expected.

JESUS: I'm glad to hear that.

2ND JOHN: He sent us to ask you: "Are you the one who is to come, or are we to wait for another?"

JESUS: Go and tell John what you hear and see: the blind receive their sight, the lame walk, the lepers are cleansed, the deaf hear, the dead are raised, and the poor have good news brought to them.

1ST JOHN: That is indeed good news.

2ND JOHN: We will take that word to John. *(Rising)* Thank you, Master.

JESUS: Oh! And one other thing. Tell him: blessed is anyone who takes no offense at me.

1ST JOHN: Yes, Master.

JOHN'S DISCIPLES give JESUS a puzzled look and leave. The two FOLLOWERS confer silently between themselves for a moment. Then they take the DISCIPLES' places.

1ST FOLL: We heard what you told those people and we think you're making a big mistake.

JESUS: I am? In what way?

2ND FOLL: We think it would be better if you were to have less to do with John.

JESUS: Oh? And why is that?

1ST FOLL: Well, John is all right, I suppose. In his place.

2ND FOLL: Yes, one expects an evangelist to rant and rave and wear funny clothes. It's all part of the game.

1ST FOLL: It works very well, actually. People come to see the show and stay to hear the message.

2ND FOLL: Attracting a crowd takes a certain amount of showmanship.

1ST FOLL: And John's certainly got it!

2ND FOLL: But ...!

JESUS: But, what?

1ST FOLL: Well, now that he's in prison ...

2ND FOLL: Exactly! It won't do your cause any good to be seen with him. Or his disciples.

1ST FOLL: And it might do a great deal of harm.

JESUS: Really? In what way?

2ND FOLL: *(Confidentially)* Well, you see, a lot of people think he's crazy.

1ST FOLL: The way he dresses!

2ND FOLL: The way he acts!

1ST FOLL: He yells at people.

2ND FOLL: And tells them they're going to hell.

1ST FOLL: People don't like that.

2ND FOLL: It puts them off.

1ST FOLL: He'll never get anyone interested in his cause that way.

2ND FOLL: He'll just alienate people from all preachers.

1ST FOLL: Including yourself.

2ND FOLL: They'll think all religious people are crazy. You don't want that, do you?

JESUS: What do you suggest?

1ST FOLL: Well, you've always been a reasonable person. That's why people like you.

2ND FOLL: You don't rant and rave.

1ST FOLL: At least not like John.

2ND FOLL: If you keep your message light — and positive. Upbeat ...

1ST FOLL: Yes! Eliminate all the doom and gloom ...

2ND FOLL: I'm sure you'll notice a big difference in the response.

1ST FOLL: People will flock to you in droves. Give them what they want to hear — love, goodness, and fellowship.

2ND FOLL: They'll eat it up.

1ST FOLL: None of that "you will be burned like chaff if you don't shape up" stuff, like John does.

JESUS: You don't like that approach?

2ND FOLL: Not at all! And I can't think of anyone else who does, either.

JESUS: But it's the truth.

1ST FOLL: That may be, but why talk about it all the time?

2ND FOLL: Most people would rather not be reminded of that sort of thing.

1ST FOLL: Right! That's where John made his big mistake.

JESUS: I see. So what you would prefer to see is someone dressed not in animal skins but in soft robes?

2ND FOLL: That would certainly be an improvement.

JESUS: And what you had hoped to hear was a reed shaken by the wind?

1ST FOLL: Well, in my opinion, he could stand to be a bit less adamant.

JESUS: Look, those who wear soft robes are in the royal palaces.

2ND FOLL: My point exactly! If John would only —

JESUS: What did you think you were seeing, there in the wilderness? A prophet? One who tells the truth, or one who tells people what they want to hear?

1ST FOLL: I don't see why he can't be a little more —

JESUS: John is a prophet. And that's what prophets do — they tell the truth. Sometimes the truth is hard to take.

1ST FOLL: It sure is! Why, just a few weeks ago, John told me —

JESUS: *(Interrupting)* But John is more than simply a prophet. This is the one about whom it is written: "See, I am sending my messenger ahead of you, Who will prepare your way before you."
Truly, I tell you, among those born of women no one has arisen greater than John the Baptist; yet the least in the kingdom of heaven is greater than he.

2ND FOLL: I don't see how that relates to his bad attitude. Perhaps the Father did send him. That doesn't mean he has to be rude about it.

1ST FOLL: Those who have a call to the religious life should be even more agreeable and pleasant than those out in the world.

2ND FOLL: That's how we know they're holy, by how nice they are. And by how many people like them.

1ST FOLL: No one sent from God could possibly alienate so many people.

2ND FOLL: It's just not ... It's just not ... NICE.

JESUS: *(Tiredly)* You're offended by him.

1ST FOLL: I certainly am! And I'm not the only one.

2ND FOLL: That's right.

JESUS: And if I were to support him you'd be offended by me.

1ST FOLL: That's what we've been trying to tell you.

2ND FOLL: It just wouldn't be in your best interests.

JESUS: What about: "Blessed is anyone who takes no offense at me?"

1ST FOLL: Well, it's not that we want to. We'd be only too happy to look upon your choices with favor.

2ND FOLL: But how can we, when you do such brainless things?

1ST FOLL: No offense.

JESUS: Perhaps you had better go find some other preacher to follow.

2ND FOLL: Does this mean you're not going to take our advice?

JESUS: I'm afraid it does.

1ST FOLL: *(To 2ND FOLLOWER)* Perhaps he's right. Perhaps we should move on. It might be for the best.

2ND FOLL: We'll find someone who's *really* nice.

1ST FOLL: *(With a look at JESUS)* And not just mouthing the words.

The two FOLLOWERS leave with backwards looks and murmurs.

JESUS: What can I say? I guess you can't please all of the people all of the time. But then, who would want to?

JESUS gets up and leaves.

What's Real?

Cast: MARY and JOSEPH

Length: 7 minutes

MARY is seated on a stool working on her embroidery. JOSEPH rushes in.

JOSEPH: Mary! Mary!

MARY: What is it, Joseph? You look all upset. Sit down and catch your breath.

JOSEPH: *(Taking a stool)* I can't wait. I'm too excited. I just had a dream.

MARY: *(Not excited)* Oh. A dream.

JOSEPH: But not just an ordinary dream. This was a special dream. This was a dream from God.

MARY: Oh! That *is* exciting.

JOSEPH: I'll say! I've never had a dream from God before. I wonder if that will happen often!

MARY: But what was the dream about?

JOSEPH: An angel appeared to me. It said, "Joseph, son of David, do not be afraid to take Mary as your wife, for the child conceived in her is from the Holy Spirit. She will bear a son and you are to name him Jesus, for he will save the people from their sins."

MARY: That's wonderful!

JOSEPH: Yes. You know what this means? We don't have to break our betrothal.

MARY: *(Smiling)* I told you we didn't.

JOSEPH: Yes. I know. You were right all along.

MARY: You didn't really doubt me, did you?

JOSEPH: Not really. But I didn't understand what was happening.

MARY: I wouldn't have understood either, except for *my* visit from the angel.

JOSEPH: I see now that all this took place in order to fulfill the prophecy:
"A virgin shall conceive and bear a son
And they shall name him Emmanuel."
(Suddenly) Hey! Wait a minute! How come the angel said to name him Jesus and not Emmanuel? There's something wrong here!

MARY: That is strange, isn't it? I wonder why that happened?

JOSEPH: I don't know. Just when everything was beginning to make sense, this has to happen.

MARY: Don't let it bother you. I'm sure there must be a good explanation.

JOSEPH: What possible explanation can there be? It's perfectly clear. The prophet said "Emmanuel" and the angel said "Jesus."

MARY: Maybe you didn't hear the angel correctly.

JOSEPH: *(Angrily)* Now you're doubting me!

MARY: Well, not exactly doubting. But you could have been mistaken.

JOSEPH: Why should I have to be the one who's mistaken? Maybe Isaiah was mistaken.

MARY: Hush! You can't say things like that about the prophet.

JOSEPH: I can say anything I like!

MARY: Joseph! Joseph! You're getting too excited.

JOSEPH: But you're accusing me of lying!

MARY: No, I'm not. I know you would never do a thing like that.

JOSEPH: Well, if I'm not lying, and the prophet's not lying, that leaves only one alternative.

MARY: I hope you're not thinking what I think you're thinking.

JOSEPH: It can only be that God is lying. No, no! That can't be right. God would never do that. *(Plaintively)* Would he?

MARY: *(Firmly)* No, he wouldn't. We just have to stay calm and think this through.

JOSEPH: This is the kind of thing that makes you wonder if the scriptures are true.

MARY: *(Shocked)* Joseph!

JOSEPH: Well, doesn't it? And this isn't the only thing. The scriptures are full of strange things. And some of them are very hard for me to believe.

MARY: Like what?

JOSEPH: Well, for instance, this business about Joshua and the walls of Jericho. He blew the horn and the walls fell down. Now, I don't know about that. Is that possible? Or the day the sun stood still so God's people could win the battle. You know that couldn't happen. That couldn't possibly happen.

MARY: It *is* pretty incredible.

JOSEPH: And the story about how ravens brought food to Elijah in the desert.

MARY: Why do you call it a "story"? I thought that was history.

JOSEPH: Do you think so? Do you *really* think so? Perhaps the writers of scripture only put that in there to convince people God can do anything.

MARY: *(Stoutly)* God *can* do anything.

JOSEPH: Perhaps we can no longer take the scriptures as trustworthy accounts of the history of our nation. Perhaps we should take a deep, long look at the historical and mythological underpinnings of our faith and admit to ourselves that its origins cannot be verified in any scientific sense.

MARY: Goodness, Joseph! I had no idea you had such doubts.

JOSEPH: Well, actually, I think it is more like a fear. *(Desperately)* What if it's not true, Mary? Have you ever thought of that? What if none of it's true?

MARY: *(Slowly)* No, I guess I've never thought of that.

JOSEPH: Think how stupid we'd look ... Think how stupid we'd *feel* if it all turned out to be a fairy tale.

MARY: *(Groans)* Oooh!

JOSEPH: Exactly! I'd be —

MARY: *(Holding her stomach)* Ahhh!

JOSEPH: Mary! What is it? Don't you feel well?

MARY: No, it's not that. Here! Put your hand here. *(She guides his hand to her stomach)*

JOSEPH: What? *(He feels it)* Oh! It's ... It's a ...

MARY: It's the baby kicking.

JOSEPH: Really! Wow! Then ... Then at least this part of it is true.

MARY: Yes, this part is true.

JOSEPH: And if this part is true — and there couldn't be a harder thing to believe than a baby without a father ...

MARY: *(Interrupting)* A baby without a *human* father.

JOSEPH: *(Nodding)* Without a human father. If that's true ... then maybe all of it is true — the ravens, and the sun standing still and ...

MARY: That's right. They could all be true. Who are we to limit God?

JOSEPH: Who indeed? I certainly apologize for having ever doubted you. And Him.

MARY: I appreciate that. And I'm sure God does, too. *(Rising)* Come on, Joseph. It's time to start dinner.

They rise and go out, arm in arm.

Very Important Persons

Cast: MARY, JOSEPH, INNKEEPER, two SHEPHERDS (may be of either gender)

Length: 15 minutes

MARY, JOSEPH and the two SHEPHERDS are seated on stools stage left. The INNKEEPER is seated on a stool stage right, watching them. There are two empty stools beside him.

MARY: *(To SHEPHERDS)* Thank you for coming. We do so much appreciate your visit.

JOSEPH: And the gifts you brought us are so practical: warm sheepskins, milk, baby clothes ...

MARY: And don't forget the diaper cloths. I don't know what we would have done without them.

JOSEPH: You shepherds have been true friends to us and our son.

1ST SHEP: We are only too glad to be of service to the new king.

2ND SHEP: It is an honor for us to be allowed to make some small contribution to his comfort.

1ST SHEP: It is an honor simply to be told of his coming. We can never thank God enough that he has allowed us to see and worship this child.

MARY: I praise God for that, as well. You are the first of all his people to know him for who he is.

JOSEPH: I hope you will not be the last.

1ST SHEP: We must be going now. But we will return with more milk and supplies tomorrow.

MARY: Thank you again, dear friends.

JOSEPH: Until tomorrow, then. *(As the SHEPHERDS leave)* And bring any others who might also wish to know him.

The SHEPHERDS exit, stage right. As they pass by the INN-KEEPER, he motions them over.

INNKEEPER: Come here, if you please, shepherds, and sit a moment.

1ST SHEP: Of course.

2ND SHEP: Is there anything we can do for you?

INNKEEPER: Yes, I think there might be. I couldn't help overhearing your conversation with these wanderers I have let stay in my barn.

1ST SHEP: *Your* barn? Oh, then you must be the innkeeper here.

INNKEEPER: Yes, I am the owner of the inn. Two nights ago these poor, bedraggled people came by, desperate for shelter. The inn was completely full, so I told them they could use the barn.

2ND SHEP: How fortunate you are then, how blessed by God, to be the one chosen to help them in their hour of need!

INNKEEPER: You think so? That's exactly what I wanted to ask you: Who *are* these people? I see shepherds from the fields coming at all hours of the day and night, bringing them gifts. Even my own wife has been out here five or six times. She's given them every extra sheet and blanket in the house. Not that I begrudge them the comfort ...

2ND SHEP: Oh, I'm sure you would not. A generous man like you!

INNKEEPER: But what I want to know is: why are you doing this? Are these important people in disguise? They don't look too important but sometimes appearances are deceiving. Perhaps the man is some high dignitary far from home and robbed of all his goods by thieves.

1ST SHEP: You're not too far wrong there, your honor.

2ND SHEP: *(Cautiously, to 1ST SHEPHERD)* But perhaps we shouldn't say. The angel never mentioned —

INNKEEPER: *(Interrupting)* Angel! What angel! What didn't it mention? What's going on here?

1ST SHEP: My friend is right. Perhaps we really shouldn't tell anyone else.

2ND SHEP: Of course, nothing was said specifically about who could and who couldn't —

INNKEEPER: *(Interrupting)* I have a right to know! This is my inn and my barn these people are sleeping in. Tell me! Right now!

1ST SHEP: *(To 2ND SHEPHERD)* Well, Joseph did say he hoped we wouldn't be the last to know.

2ND SHEP: That's true. And he told us to bring anyone else who wished to know him.

INNKEEPER: *(Beside himself with impatience)* Him? Who's him? Tell me! I have to know.

1ST SHEP: Well, all right. *(Solemnly)* This child, the child who was born night before last in your barn, is the Messiah, the Chosen One of Israel.

INNKEEPER: You're kidding!

2ND SHEP: No, really! This is he of whom the prophet spoke: "For unto us a child is born, unto us a son is given."

INNKEEPER: But this can't be!

1ST SHEP: Why not?

INNKEEPER: Because! Because they ... they look so ordinary!

2ND SHEP: There's nothing wrong with ordinary.

INNKEEPER: How do you know all this, anyway?

1ST SHEP: Well, you see, two nights ago, as we were tending our flocks in the fields just out of town, an angel of the Lord appeared before us, and the glory of the Lord shone round us ...

2ND SHEP: And we were terrified!

1ST SHEP: But the angel said to us: "Do not be afraid, for see — I am bringing you good news of great joy for all the people: To you is born this day in the city of David, a Savior who is the Messiah, the Lord."

2ND SHEP: And then it told us where to find him: "Wrapped in swaddling clothes and lying in a manger."

1ST SHEP: Then suddenly there was with the angel a multitude of the heavenly host, praising God and saying: "Glory to God in the highest and on earth peace to those of good will."

INNKEEPER: Wow!

1ST SHEP: Exactly!

INNKEEPER: *(After a moment)* You realize what this means.

2ND SHEP: Of course. It means that we no longer need to fear death and sin.

1ST SHEP: As the prophet said: The yoke of our burden has been lifted from us.

INNKEEPER: And the rod of the oppressor has been broken.

2ND SHEP: Ah! I see you know your scripture.

INNKEEPER: Of course! "For all the boots of the tramping warriors and all the garments rolled in blood shall be burned as fuel for the fire." Isaiah 9:5

1ST SHEP: *(Cautiously)* It does say that.

INNKEEPER: And "He shall multiply the nation." *Our* nation. At his coming we shall exult as people do when dividing plunder.

2ND SHEP: That's true. *(Glancing nervously at 1ST SHEPHERD)* I suppose.

INNKEEPER: Of course it's true. At last our nation can triumph over her enemies! At last we can rid ourselves of the profaners and blasphemers who are running this country!

1ST SHEP: Er ...

INNKEEPER: *(Excited)* After all these years of subjugation and humiliation we can regain our rightful heritage and once again become a God-fearing nation! "For the government will be upon *his* shoulders!"

2ND SHEP: I ... don't ...

INNKEEPER: *(Shaking their hands vigorously)* Thank you! Thank you for telling me this wonderful news! But I must run! There's so much work to be done.

The INNKEEPER jumps off his stool and rushes over to sit beside JOSEPH and MARY. The SHEPHERDS get slowly off their stools and leave, looking back occasionally as if unsure if they should go.

INNKEEPER: Excuse me! Are you the parents of this wonderful child?

JOSEPH: We are.

MARY: Have you come to worship?

INNKEEPER: Of course. But more than that, I've come to help.

MARY: Thank you. We certainly appreciate that. Your wife has been very kind.

INNKEEPER: I should hope so! Well, the first thing is to get you out of this barn and into my finest room.

JOSEPH: But I though your inn was completely full.

INNKEEPER: Oh, it is. It is. But I'll kick somebody out.

MARY: *(Looking at JOSEPH)* I don't think we could do that.

INNKEEPER: It wouldn't be any trouble at all.

JOSEPH: Definitely not!

INNKEEPER: But we can't have the Messiah living in a barn. What would people say?

JOSEPH: Which people?

45

INNKEEPER: The people who can do you the most good. The first thing is to get organized. And I can help with that. A good innkeeper has all the skills necessary to make it in today's world — to deal well with people, to get the word out to potential customers, to collect a decent staff ...

MARY: Staff?

INNKEEPER: Of course! We'll need politically astute people on our side to establish a dialogue between us and the present rulers of the country.

JOSEPH: To what end?

INNKEEPER: To negotiate for the transfer of power.

JOSEPH and MARY stare at him in dismay.

INNKEEPER: The prophet did say: "The government shall be upon his shoulders," didn't he?

JOSEPH: Well, yes. But —

INNKEEPER: At the very least, we have to make sure our concerns are being addressed by those higher up. We want to maintain access to the present centers of power. Wouldn't you agree?

JOSEPH: I'm not sure —

INNKEEPER: Please! You must not ignore the clear meaning of the prophecies. This child is destined to be our ruler, to return our nation to its former way of life, and to give those of us who are God-fearing a greater say in the way things are done around here. I assume you will be acting as his regent until he is of age.

JOSEPH: I'll be acting as his parent.

INNKEEPER: My dear sir. I hope you won't let your lowly station in life blind you to your present obligations. The Messiah's cause will be ill served by a naive approach to the realities of politics. His very existence is a threat to those who wish to squander the resources of this holy nation in pursuit of their own purposes. There will be many who will do everything in their power to thwart him.

JOSEPH: Yes, I understand that.

INNKEEPER: His ascendancy must be our first concern. We cannot let our enemies continue to turn a nation founded on the principles of scripture and the will of God into a cesspool of self-centered, undisciplined ...

JOSEPH: The will of God, for us, is —

INNKEEPER: *(Interrupting)* Of primary importance. I appreciate that. And I'm sure you'll agree that it is God's will that we guard our precious heritage. Our greatest commitment must be to the children. We can't allow them to grow up in the kind of godless environment our enemies are trying to impose. I fear for the children. I fear for their minds and more — for their very souls.

MARY: Well, naturally —

INNKEEPER: It would be criminal for us to let another year go by, nay, another month, without attempting to reverse the insidious secular influence forced upon us by those who have no regard for the principles upon which this nation was founded.

JOSEPH:	We do realize, of course, that the Roman occupation has made it easy for many to abandon their commitment to God. But a position of neutrality, at least for the present —
INNKEEPER:	Neutrality! My dear sir! The very word should be repugnant to you! That is exactly why we are in the position we're in, why the God-fearing institutions in this land are so impotent. A neutral approach is useless. Worse than useless; it is pathetic! Next you'll be suggesting we talk to them.
JOSEPH:	Talking couldn't do —
INNKEEPER:	You're absolutely right! It couldn't possibly do any good. These people aren't listening to us. Nor do they have any intention of doing so. We can approach them only from a position of power. And there is power in numbers. Never forget that. Sixty-two percent of this country claim to be God-fearing. We have the data to back that up. It should be one hundred percent, of course, but years of the enemy's influence have taken their toll.
MARY:	But, sir —
INNKEEPER:	The present government's policies are horribly detrimental to the well-being of our families — the future of this country. We cannot simply stand back and let that happen.
JOSEPH:	I'm sure God must have his own plans for that. But first of all, our people must change their way of thinking and change their hearts.

INNKEEPER: Change? Change? It's not we who must change. This nation was founded on scriptural truth and scriptural truth is reality and cannot be changed. To be anti-truth is to be anti-God!

MARY: I'm sure Joseph didn't mean —

INNKEEPER: It is they who must change or we will throw them out! Let us not lose sight of the gravity of the harm done by this administration's promulgation of sinful laws and loathsome lifestyles. What this country needs is a godly leader. Now! And this child is the one. He can do great things for this nation. With us behind him, of course.

JOSEPH: *(Sarcastically)* Of course!

MARY: But that's not God's plan.

INNKEEPER: No? Then what is?

MARY: *(Bravely)* I don't know, but I'm pretty sure that's not it.

INNKEEPER: Scripture says he will rule this land. It says that he will uphold the throne of David with justice and with righteousness and that there will be endless peace. Are you willing to go against the clear meaning of Scripture? Are you willing to deprive your own people of such tremendous benefits?

MARY: Well ... no. But I think there are better ways to accomplish God's will.

INNKEEPER: For instance?

MARY: Well, prayer, for instance.

INNKEEPER: Prayer? Prayer! A lot of good that is going to do against godless people.

MARY: What do you mean?

INNKEEPER: Prayer only works for those who believe. You and I might be influenced by prayer, but it hardly influences the leaders of this country.

JOSEPH: You don't believe God can do that?

INNKEEPER: Of course I believe that. But still, if he wanted to, wouldn't he have done so by now? No, he needs us to bring this about. We are an essential part of his plan. *(Piously)* Remember, "He has no hands but ours."

JOSEPH: It would be more interesting to watch him do it without us, though. Wouldn't it?

INNKEEPER: *(Disgustedly)* Well, if you're willing to abandon your responsibilities like that, fine! But I have more of a conscience. Give me the child and I'll take care of the whole thing myself.

MARY: *(Appalled)* No!

The INNKEEPER starts toward the crib and JOSEPH stands in his way. Just then the two SHEPHERDS enter and the INNKEEPER, realizing he is outnumbered, allows JOSEPH and the 1ST SHEPHERD to lead him away. The 2ND SHEPHERD takes a seat beside MARY.

2ND SHEP: We were a little worried about leaving you alone with him, so we came back.

MARY: I'm glad you did.

2ND SHEP: There've been rumors about him in our camp. This isn't the first time he's made trouble. He not only objects to the Romans but calls any Jew he disagrees with horrible names, and tells them they are going to hell. He has a hard time relating to those who don't think exactly like he does.

MARY: I'm afraid that includes Joseph and me.

2ND SHEP: Yes, well, there will always be people like that. People who think they know better than God.

JOSEPH and the 1ST SHEPHERD enter. JOSEPH takes the stool next to MARY and puts his arm around her. The 1ST SHEPHERD stands beside him.

JOSEPH: Perhaps God just isn't doing things fast enough to satisfy them and they've decided to try to speed things up a bit.

MARY: Yes. I think all those wonderful things the prophet spoke about will come true, someday. But we might have a bit of waiting to do.

JOSEPH: *(Looking at the child)* Yes. Let it be all in his own good time.

2ND SHEP: Amen!

Great Africans Of The Bible: Simon Of Cyrene

Cast: SIMON of Cyrene, a middle-aged Black man, and his two young sons, ALEXANDER and RUFUS

Length: 9 minutes

SIMON is seated on the middle stool of three, flanked by his sons.

SIMON: Did I ever tell you boys about the time I saw the Son of God?

RUFUS: No! Did you really?

ALEX: Oh, Dad! Tell us what it was like. Did you hear him preach?

SIMON: No, Alexander. I only saw him once and it was at the saddest time of his life. It was the day he was crucified.

ALEX: You were there?

RUFUS: That must have been awesome!

SIMON: It was.

ALEX: Were you already a believer then?

SIMON: No, Alex, I wasn't. I didn't even know who this man was. I don't know why I stayed to watch. I was new in town, I had just come from Africa, and I wanted to see everything that was going on in Jerusalem. I was just walking along, enjoying the sights, when I saw that the soldiers had blocked off the street ahead. A condemned man — a dissenter, according to the guy next to me — was coming through on his way to the execution site. I had seen how the Romans treated dissenters in Cyrene and I knew it would be pretty bad.

ALEX: How bad was it?

SIMON: As bad as anything I've ever seen.

RUFUS: What do they do to dissenters, Dad?

ALEX: What *is* a dissenter, Dad?

SIMON: A dissenter is someone who complains about the way things are. The Romans don't like anyone complaining. Especially if they make other people feel the same way.

RUFUS: Was he complaining about the way the Romans treated the Jews?

SIMON: No. That was the funny thing. He wasn't complaining about the Romans at all. He was complaining about the other Jews, the religious leaders.

ALEX: The other Jews! But then why did the Romans kill him?

SIMON: Apparently, the religious leaders had told the Romans that this fellow was claiming to be the king of Judea. The Romans didn't like that. Caesar wanted to be king and he didn't appreciate any competition.

RUFUS: What did they do to him?

SIMON: They put him to death, the Roman way, nailed to a cross.

RUFUS: Eewww!

ALEX: That must have hurt.

SIMON: Yes, Alex, I'm sure it did. First they took him to the police station and grilled him all night, trying to get him to confess.

ALEX: Did he confess?

RUFUS: He couldn't confess because he hadn't done anything. That's right, isn't it, Dad?

SIMON: That's right, Rufus. When they questioned him, he didn't say anything at all. Then they beat him with metal-tipped thongs and put big thorns into his head. And then they made him carry his own cross up to the crucifixion site.

ALEX: That's bad.

SIMON: Yes, it was. He was in a lot of pain. The cross was so heavy he could barely manage it. He fell three times. The first two times he pulled himself up again and struggled on.

RUFUS: What happened the third time?

SIMON: That time when he fell, he couldn't get up again. He just lay there, panting, the sweat and blood running off his face into the dirt.

RUFUS: Didn't he even try?

SIMON: Oh, he tried, all right. But he was just too worn out. They had been beating him all night and he was a mess.

ALEX: Then what happened?

SIMON: One of the guards turned around and looked into the crowd. He pointed at me. "You!" he said. "Get over here and help this man."

RUFUS: But why did he pick you, Dad?

ALEX: Was it because he thought you weren't a Jew?

SIMON: That might have been part of it.

RUFUS: Was it because you were dark-skinned?

SIMON: That might have been part of it, too. But I think it was also because I was so big and strong. Some of the men in that crowd couldn't have picked up one little corner of that cross.

RUFUS: That was really unfair!

SIMON: That's what I thought at the time.

ALEX: You must have been mad that you got picked.

SIMON: I was. Believe me, I was! I was as good a Jew as any other in the crowd. That's what I told myself. I didn't deserve that kind of treatment just because I was from Africa. I cursed and swore all the way up that hill. I cursed at the Romans and I cursed at God.

RUFUS: I would have done that, too.

SIMON: I hope not, Rufus, because I was wrong.

RUFUS: You were?

SIMON: Yes. Being made to carry his cross was the best thing that ever happened to me.

RUFUS: It was?

SIMON: Yes. Because as we were going up the hill, he started talking to me.

ALEX: Jesus talked to you? Just to you?

SIMON: He did. And what he said changed my life forever.

RUFUS: What did he say, Dad?

SIMON: Well, at first, I did most of the talking. I was cursing and swearing and threatening to kill that guard if I ever got the chance. I was moaning on about how unfair life was, and then he said, "Yes, it is, isn't it?"

RUFUS: That's not very profound.

SIMON: No, but it made me stop and think. Here was this poor guy who was innocent to all the charges against him and yet he was about to be put to death. It made my own problems look pretty small in comparison.

RUFUS: Still ...!

SIMON: I asked him if he never felt like killing the people who had done that to him.

RUFUS: What did he say?

SIMON: He said that mostly he felt sorry for them.

RUFUS: Sorry! But they had all the power!

SIMON: I'm not sure about that. As he said, it's a lot harder not to hate. And a lot better for your soul. I asked him — rather sarcastically, I'm afraid — what he knew about souls.

RUFUS: What did he say?

SIMON: He quoted scripture to me.

ALEX: *He* must have known you were a Jew.

SIMON: I think he knew everything about me. He knew how angry I was at the Romans, and how bitter I was about the way they had treated people I cared about in Cyrene. He knew that I was ready to kill them. And he was right. I would have. I hated them.

RUFUS: *(Beside himself with impatience)* Dad! What — did — he — say?

SIMON: He said, "Vengeance is mine, sayeth the Lord." I said, "I'd rather do it myself." Then he said, "Don't you trust God to do the right thing?" And I realized then that, no, I didn't. I didn't trust God to take care of it. Not the way I would like to see it taken care of, with all the Romans hurting or dead. And very, very sorry they ever messed with me.

ALEX: Wow!

SIMON: He saw right through my fear and anger and saw to the heart of the matter, that I didn't want God to take my hatred away from me. I liked it, and I wanted to keep on hating because I thought that would make me stronger and keep the Romans away from the people I loved.

ALEX: But it didn't?

SIMON: No. The only thing anger and hatred do is what had been done to Jesus: an innocent man was tortured and put to death. And for what? *(Pause)* Later, during those terrible hours he was hanging on the cross, half-dead, in awful pain, I talked to some of his friends. They told me who he was and what he had been teaching. That's the day I became a believer.

RUFUS: But still ...! Wouldn't you have killed a Roman if they came after you?

SIMON: Maybe. I don't know. But I do know that the hatred I was feeling was far worse for me than death ever could be.

RUFUS: Really?

SIMON: *(Smiling)* Really! The things we do on this earth only take on their proper perspective when you see them in relation to the eternal life Jesus has promised us. Then we understand that God's way is the best way. Now I leave things like vengeance up to him.

RUFUS: But does he ever do anything about it?

SIMON: Perhaps. Perhaps not. What does it matter?

RUFUS: I guess it doesn't. Not if you look at it that way.

SIMON: Take my word for it, Rufus. God's way is the best way. Perhaps some day you'll be chosen to do some great deed for God, like I was.

RUFUS: *(Seriously)* I'd like that.

SIMON: So would I. The day I was chosen to carry His cross was the happiest day of my life. *(Getting down from his stool)* Come on, let's go get some ice cream.

ALEX: Okay!

RUFUS: Great!

ALEX and RUFUS run out and SIMON follows them.

1996

Repentance

Cast: FRED and ELLEN

Length: 4 minutes

FRED and ELLEN are sitting on their stools.

FRED: I'd really like to confess my sins and receive God's forgiveness, but I'm afraid they're much too awful. I'm sure He wouldn't be interested.

ELLEN: That's not true. Nothing's so awful that God won't forgive it.

FRED: My sins are.

ELLEN: No, no! You don't understand! God's gracious and merciful, slow to anger and rich in kindness.

FRED: He won't be after He hears what I've done.

ELLEN: No, really. As long as you're truly sorry, God is willing to forgive. *(Pause)* Er, Fred. It's probably none of my business, but what was it that ...? No, no! I shouldn't ask.

FRED: Don't. It's too terrible. So terrible I know I can never be forgiven.

ELLEN: I can't believe there's anything God wouldn't forgive.

FRED: You have no idea! Just the thought of the punishment He'll hand out is enough to make me cringe.

ELLEN: You're not listening to me, Fred. God doesn't punish that way. You'll be forgiven if you're truly sorry.

FRED: No, you're wrong. I know there's no reprieve. I'll be lucky to escape with my life.

ELLEN: Fred! You have to tell me. What did you do?

FRED: *(Thinks about it, then rejects the idea)* No. I can't tell. It's too horrible.

ELLEN: Maybe I can help you.

FRED: I already know the verdict. There's nothing anyone can do for me now.

ELLEN: Look! I'll pray for you. You'll see how easy it is. Spare, O God, this poor fellow Fred, who thinks he's done something unforgivable.

FRED: I don't just think so. It *is* unforgivable!

ELLEN: There's nothing that's unforgivable. What is it? Tell me, and I'll show you how wrong you are.

FRED: All right. I smashed up your car.

ELLEN: *(Staring at him)* You're kidding!

FRED: Hear, O God, the prayer of your servant. Spare me from retribution ...

ELLEN: *(Grimly)* That's not going to help you now.

FRED: *(Louder)* Hear, O Lord, my prayer! Protect me from the wrath ...

ELLEN: God's not going to protect you, so you might as well give it up.

FRED: But I thought you said that if I were truly sorry ...

ELLEN: You were right the first time. Some things *are* unforgivable.

FRED: What about mercy and kindness? What about slow to anger?

ELLEN: That's only for offenses against God. This one's against *me*!

FRED: I think I'd rather have God mad at me than you.

ELLEN: You'd be better off. *Much* better off!

FRED: You're not very much like God, are you? He would forgive. He would show mercy.

ELLEN: No, I ... I mean I ... *(Pause)* No. I guess I'm not. *(Defiantly)* But I don't have to be.

FRED: Don't you? Isn't that the whole point? Aren't we supposed to forgive as God does?

ELLEN: Well, I suppose you're right. And you've certainly done the proper amount of weeping and mourning for your sins. All right! I forgive you.

FRED: That's great, because there's one other thing ...

ELLEN: *(Putting her hands over her ears)* No! Don't tell me! I don't want to hear! Confess your sins to God. He can handle them. I can't!

She runs offstage, her hands still over her ears. FRED smiles at the audience, shrugs, picks up both stools and follows her off.

Before The Fall

Cast: EVE, ADAM, and GOD

Length: 8 minutes

The person playing GOD is sitting alone in the center of the room. He turns to look off to the right and calls to two people out of sight of the audience.

GOD: Adam. Eve. Could you come here? I'd like to talk to you for a moment.

ADAM: *(Hurrying in, carrying a stool)* Yes, God?

EVE: *(Following him, with stool)* What is it, God?

GOD: You see what a beautiful garden I've created for your home. Are you happy here?

EVE: Oh, yes, Lord! It's lovely.

ADAM: We're very happy here.

GOD: Good! I want you to be happy.

ADAM: You're very gracious, Lord. You've given us everything we could possibly want.

EVE: Everything. Except ...

ADAM: *(To EVE)* Hush, now! You sound ungrateful.

65

GOD: No. Tell me, Eve. I want to know. Is there something else I could do for you?

EVE: *(Slowly)* Well, there is one thing. Something that would make us happier than all the rest.

GOD: Yes? What is it?

ADAM: We'd like the opportunity to somehow repay You for all You've done for us.

GOD: Repay Me? But you don't have to do that. All I've given you has been a gift. Free. No strings attached.

ADAM: I realize that. But still, we'd feel better if we could do something to ... to ...

GOD: *(Suspiciously)* To earn it?

EVE: No. Not exactly *earn* it. But to show how much we appreciate Your marvellous generosity.

ADAM: Will You give us that chance?

GOD: You couldn't just take it as a gift and leave it at that?

ADAM: It wouldn't seem right, somehow.

EVE: It would make us uncomfortable.

GOD: *(Doubtfully)* Well, if you're really sure ...

ADAM: Yes, we are. Naming the animals was fun, but that's all over now.

EVE: We're very sure. Tending the garden is great, but it's not all that important.

GOD: Well, I suppose it's only right that you should have a try. But do you really think you can handle it?

ADAM: Oh, yes! Positive.

EVE: Nothing would give us greater pleasure.

ADAM: Just tell us what You want us to do and stand back!

GOD: All right then. But first let me explain that I'm not asking anything impossible.

ADAM: We're not going to change our minds, if that's what You're worried about. We will carry on, no matter how difficult the task!

EVE: Not even if we have to walk a hundred miles on our hands and knees!

ADAM: Not even if we have to fight wild beasts barehanded!

EVE: Not if we have to put hot coals in our mouths!

GOD: *(Wryly)* I'm afraid it won't be quite as dramatic as all that. *(Points)* Do you see that tall tree in the center of the garden?

ADAM: The one with the apples?

GOD: Yes. That is the Tree of the Knowledge of Good and Evil. I don't want you to eat any of that tree's fruit. Not one piece. You can eat of the fruit of any other tree in this garden, but not that one.

EVE: And then?

GOD: That's it. Just don't eat that fruit. Do you think you can manage?

ADAM: That's all? No wild beasts?

EVE: No hot coals? No walking on our knees?

GOD: Nope.

EVE: *(Pouting)* But that's no fun!

ADAM: Eve's right! It's too easy! We wanted to do something hard — to show You how much we appreciate what You've done for us.

GOD: Believe Me, if you can do that much, it will be plenty.

ADAM: Sure! No sweat! I could do that with my eyes closed.

EVE: With one hand tied behind my back.

ADAM: Piece of cake! But are You sure we couldn't, say, scale the highest mountain? Or plumb the watery depths?

GOD: Just do this and you'll make me very happy.

He leaves.

ADAM: Well, that's what we wanted, wasn't it?

EVE: I guess so. But it seems so ... so *passive*, so useless, so unimportant.

ADAM: *(Gloomily)* Not terribly thrilling.

EVE: Why do you suppose he picked that particular tree?

ADAM: I don't know. Maybe because it was the tallest.

EVE: It doesn't look all that special.

ADAM: What does it matter? It's just a tree.

EVE: God said it was the Tree of the Knowledge of Good and Evil. What could that possibly mean?

ADAM: You know how it is. He's got names for everything. It's probably just a ... er, ... Or a ...

EVE: *(Scornfully)* You don't have the slightest idea what it's all about, do you?

ADAM: No, and I don't care. If God said don't eat, I don't eat!

EVE: You're such a goody-goody! A push-over! You'll do anything anyone tells you. Until the next person comes along and tells you something different.

ADAM: *(Angrily)* Listen! You were the one who asked God what you could do to make Him happy. This wasn't my idea, you know.

EVE: So now it's *my* idea! I thought you were the one who wasn't happy here.

ADAM: I'm plenty happy! I just thought we could be happier.

EVE: Well, I'm happy, too! Terrifically happy! Just as I am.

ADAM: Fine! We're both happy. But, you know, there's something else about this situation I don't like. It makes me nervous, always being on the receiving end of things. Don't you feel that way, too? I'd like to know that what I do has some value, too.

EVE: Yeah! I know what you mean. He's always the one who gives, and we're always the ones who take. It shouldn't be like that.

ADAM: I'd feel better about it if I knew there was something we had that He wanted.

EVE: Or needed.

ADAM: Right! Of course, there is. He told us He wanted us not to eat that fruit. I suppose you could say He *needed* us not to eat that fruit.

EVE: But how could it be that important? It just doesn't seem very satisfying for some reason, does it?

ADAM: No. It doesn't. Maybe that's because it's not a real job. It's not something we could do for Him that He'd really be grateful for.

EVE: Yeah! It's like a made-up thing. Not really important.

ADAM: I wish we could do something *really* important.

EVE: Then *we'd* be more important. More like HIM.

ADAM: Instead of being just ... *dependents*!

EVE: I *hate* being dependent!

ADAM: Me too! It's so *demeaning*! I want to be able to *earn* my way.

EVE: Yeah! Pay for what we get. Not have to take it from Him as a stupid gift! A gift we can never really repay.

ADAM: I agree! But I don't know that there's anything we can do about it. He's got this whole Paradise thing arranged all His way.

EVE: *(Thoughtfully)* Maybe not. This serpent I met recently was telling me ...

ADAM: You and your serpent! Can't you find someone a little more ... well, someone from a higher species to talk to?

EVE: There's nothing wrong with serpents! You're just jealous because I spend more time with him than with you.

ADAM: I really don't care how you spend your time. I've got more important things to do. Spend all day with your serpent, if that's what makes you happy!

He stomps off, taking his stool with him.

EVE: *(Yelling after him)* Fine! If you're going to be like that, I will! *(Looks off stage)* Oh, serpent! *(Begins walking off, talking as she goes)* Do you happen to know anything that God really needs? Because we'd like to figure out some way to pay him back for all the ...

1996

Reading Between
The Lines

Cast: JESUS and NICODEMUS

Length: 7 minutes

JESUS is seated on one of two stools center stage. NICODE-
MUS enters furtively and takes the other stool.

NICO: Rabbi Jesus, if you don't mind, there are a few questions I've been dying to ask you.

JESUS: Of course, Nicodemus. Ask away.

NICO: Well, some of my fellow Pharisees believe you are
from Satan. But there are some of us who believe
you are a teacher sent to us from God.

JESUS: Thank you. I appreciate that.

NICO: It seems perfectly logical. No one can do these signs
that you do apart from the presence of God.

JESUS: True. But that's not what you came to see me about,
is it?

NICO: It's not?

JESUS: No. What you really want to know is: How does
one enter into the kingdom of heaven.

NICO: Not necessarily. I've read the scriptures. I know what I need to do.

JESUS: Do you?

NICO: Yes. I know what to do and I've done it. I've spent my whole life obeying the law, every tiniest aspect of it. And I'm sure God will count me among the righteous.

JESUS: Well, then, I'm sure you don't need me to tell you any more.

NICO: No, please! I'd like to hear what you have to say. Just out of curiosity.

JESUS: Well, I'm sure you learned in your studies of scripture that no one can enter the kingdom of God without having been born again.

NICO: Born again? I never read anything about that. Besides, it doesn't even make sense! How can anyone be born again after having grown old? Can one enter a second time into the mother's womb?

JESUS: Please don't take me so literally, Nicodemus. I was using a metaphor.

NICO: Oh. Sorry.

JESUS: This is the truth. No one can enter the kingdom of God without being born of water and Spirit.

NICO: *(Interrupting)* But —!

JESUS: *(Holding up his hand for silence)* Wait! Let me explain. What is born of the flesh is flesh, and what is born of the Spirit is Spirit. We're not talking here about your body but about your spirit.

74

NICO: But I still —!

JESUS: *(Interrupting)* I don't know why you are so astonished when I say to you, "You must be born again." Only God's grace can grant us entrance into his kingdom.

NICO: Not only am I astonished, I'm confused. What you say doesn't make any sense. How will I be able to manage this rebirth you say is so necessary?

JESUS: But that's the whole point. You don't have to.

NICO: What?

JESUS: I realize this is hard to understand. Perhaps I can use another metaphor to make it clearer. Let's compare the movement of the Spirit to the wind. The wind blows where it chooses. You hear the sound of it but you do not know where it comes from or where it goes. So it is with everyone who is born of the spirit.

NICO: Are you saying that the Spirit arranges this rebirth?

JESUS: Yes.

NICO: And the Spirit is like the wind, coming and going where it pleases?

JESUS: Yes.

NICO: So the Spirit moves *randomly*?

JESUS: No, not randomly. Just not predictably. And certainly not under anyone's control.

NICO: *(Frustrated)* But I don't understand! How can these things be?

JESUS: I don't understand why you can't understand. You are a teacher of Israel; you have read the scriptures, and yet you still do not see what I'm talking about?

NICO: What you're saying goes against everything I've ever learned. I thought I knew what I needed to do and now you're telling me there's something else?

JESUS: Not something else. The same things that were there all along.

NICO: *(Shaking his head)* I don't know.

JESUS: You said you believed I was sent from God. Then trust me to tell you the truth.

NICO: I don't know if I can. I don't know if I should.

JESUS: You have heard all that my disciples and I have been doing and saying. Let me assure you that we speak of what we know and testify to what we have seen. Yet you still do not receive our testimony.

NICO: It just seems so strange.

JESUS: If I have told you about earthly things and you do not believe, how can you believe if I tell you about heavenly things? Could it be that you don't want to hear?

NICO: *(Indignantly)* Of course I do! I was the one who came here to ask you questions. Why would I do that if I didn't want to hear?

JESUS: Then trust me. You were right, I do come from God. No one has ascended into heaven except the one who descended from heaven, the Son of Man.

NICO: And that one is you?

JESUS: That's right. I know what the Father wants from you. And what he wants is for you to trust him and allow the Spirit to bring you into a new life.

NICO: Even if it doesn't make sense?

JESUS: Yes.

NICO: Even if it isn't in scripture?

JESUS: Scripture has always claimed that only God's mercy can bring salvation.

NICO: What you want is for me to trust God blindly.

JESUS: If that's what it takes, yes.

NICO: And you want me to trust you blindly when you say you speak for him.

JESUS: That's right.

NICO: That's really hard. I don't know whether I can do this.

JESUS: I agree. It is hard.

NICO: You're asking me to give up my whole way of life, to admit that everything I've done up 'til now has been wasted effort.

JESUS: Not completely. You've been a good teacher, based on what you understood. And you've tried honestly to please your Father in heaven. But now God is asking you to look at things a whole new way. His way.

NICO: Still, I'd have to give up everything I've worked so hard for — my position among the Pharisees, my teaching job — you know they'll never let me stay if I let on that I've become one of your followers. I'll lose my credibility, my reputation. And all for ... All for ...

JESUS: Eternal life. *(Pause)* Is it worth it?

NICO: Of course it is! *(Pause)* And yet ...

NICODEMUS gets up, shaking his head, and slowly walks out, staring at the floor. JESUS watches him sadly, then he gets up and slowly walks out in the opposite direction.

1996

God Quenches Our Thirst

Cast: JESUS, SAMARITAN WOMAN

Length: 5 minutes

JESUS enters, carrying his stool, and sits down next to the SAMARITAN WOMAN.

JESUS: Excuse me. I am thirsty. Will you give me a drink from the well?

WOMAN: You ask that of me, a Samaritan? And a woman?

JESUS: Why not? Is that too much to ask? You have a bucket on a rope long enough to reach the water. I do not.

WOMAN: You don't understand. It's not a matter of who's got the bucket. It's a matter of custom.

JESUS: What custom?

WOMAN: Women are not allowed to speak to .... That is, no man would .... Oh, never mind. Here! Hold this cup while I fill it.

They mime pouring and receiving water.

JESUS: *(Drinks)* Thank you. *(He hands back the cup)* If you knew all God had to give, and knew who it was that was asking you for water, you would have asked him instead for the Living Water. And he would have given it to you.

WOMAN: Where would you get this living water? You have nothing to draw water with and the well is deep.

JESUS: The Living Water does not come from this well. Whoever drinks from this well will be thirsty again. But whoever drinks the water I will give will never thirst. The water I give is like a fountain within you, springing up to provide you with eternal life.

WOMAN: Sir, give me some of this water so I will never grow thirsty again.

JESUS: I will. Sit down here beside me and I will tell you all about it.

WOMAN: *(Peering at him suspiciously)* You are a most remarkable man.

JESUS: How is that?

WOMAN: You are a Jew. Yet you ask me, a woman and a Samaritan, for a drink. And then to sit and talk. That's not usually done.

JESUS: Things are changing. What was the custom before will be the custom no longer.

WOMAN: Really? There will be a lot of people who won't like that.

JESUS: Which people?

WOMAN: People who don't like change. People who want things to stay the same as they are.

JESUS: Yes, I can imagine that some of the changes that are coming will upset those people. How will you feel about them?

WOMAN: Me? Oh, I like change. I get bored if things stay the same too long.

JESUS: Well, one can go too far in the opposite direction.

WOMAN: I beg your pardon?

JESUS: Change is good only if it is change for the better.

WOMAN: I suppose that's true. What are these changes you've been talking about? Besides Jews talking to Samaritans and men talking to women.

JESUS: Well, for one thing, the time is coming when you will worship the Father neither on this mountain nor in Jerusalem.

WOMAN: Wow! That's a pretty big change. I *know* the Samaritan leaders are not going to like that.

JESUS: Still, it will happen. An hour is coming, actually, it is already here, when authentic worshippers will worship the Father in Spirit and in Truth. Indeed, it is just such worshippers the Father seeks. God is Spirit and those who worship him must worship in Spirit and in Truth.

WOMAN: That's pretty complicated. I'm not sure I understand.

JESUS: If you like, I'll explain further.

81

WOMAN: Great!

JESUS: Would you like me to explain it to your husband as well? I'll wait while you go get him.

WOMAN: Sir, I have no husband.

JESUS: That's right. In fact, you have had five. And the man you are living with now is not your husband.

WOMAN: How did you know that? You must be from God! What else can you tell me?

JESUS: I can tell you more about the changes that are coming. For too long you have worshipped the Father without knowing what it is he wants from you.

WOMAN: And you know what it is the Father wants from me? *I* don't even know what he wants from me.

JESUS: Are you sure?

WOMAN: Well, I suppose I do. I suppose he might like it if I stopped changing husbands just because I get bored. Or because they no longer suit me.

JESUS: That's right. The time has come for you to worship with understanding.

WOMAN: But it's not always easy to know what the Father wants. The Jews say one thing and our own leaders say another. It's so confusing! I know there is a Messiah coming. Perhaps when he comes he will explain things so that we can understand.

82

JESUS: He will. And I who speak to you am he.

WOMAN: *(Kneeling to him)* My Lord! I believe you *are* the Savior of the World! You know so much about me. Only the Messiah could know that. Only the Messiah would tell me the truth.

JESUS: *(Helping her rise)* Daughter, your faith has saved you.

WOMAN: Let me tell all the people of my village! They will want to hear what you have to say.

JESUS: Go ahead. I will follow.

They leave together.

Whose Fault?

Cast: JESUS, JAMES, JOHN, BLIND MAN, 1ST PHARISEE, 2ND PHARISEE, MOTHER, FATHER

Length: 7 minutes

The BLIND MAN is seated on the fourth of eight stools. JESUS, JAMES and JOHN enter and sit near him, JESUS closest to the BLIND MAN and the other two next to JESUS.

JOHN: This man is blind. I understand he has been blind from birth.

JAMES: *(To JESUS)* Rabbi, was it his own sin or his parents' that caused him to be born this way?

JESUS: Neither! It was no sin that caused this, either of this man or his parents. Rather, it was to let God's work show forth in him.

JAMES: But, how can that be? How can God be glorified by this man's blindness?

JESUS stoops to the ground and mimes picking up a handful of earth and spitting on it. He then smears the man's face with the mud.

JAMES: Lord! What are you doing?

JESUS: *(To the BLIND MAN)* Go, wash your face in the pool of Siloam.

The BLIND MAN leaves.

JESUS: We must do the deeds of him who sent me while it is day. The night comes on when no one can work.

JOHN: What work are you talking about, Lord?

JESUS: While I am in the world, I am the light of the world.

JAMES: *(To JOHN)* Do you understand what he means?

JOHN shakes his head. The BLIND MAN returns, followed by two PHARISEES.

BLIND MAN: I can see! I can see! *(Bowing to JESUS)* Thank you, Master!

He takes his seat and the others take the stools on his far side.

1ST PHARISEE: *(To the other PHARISEE)* Isn't this the fellow who used to sit and beg by the city gate?

2ND PHARISEE: It sure looks like him. But this man isn't blind, so it must be someone else.

BLIND MAN: No. It's me, all right! I was blind, but now I see.

2ND PHARISEE: How did it happen? How were your eyes opened?

BLIND MAN: This man *(Indicating JESUS)* they call Jesus made mud and smeared it on my eyes, telling me to go to Siloam and wash. When I did go and wash, I was able to see. He must be from God.

1ST PHARISEE: No, that's not right. He can't be from God.

2ND PHARISEE: Why not?

1ST PHARISEE: Because if he were from God, he wouldn't have healed him on the Sabbath. Godly people always keep the Sabbath. Therefore, he isn't from God. He is only a sinner and sinners can't heal. Besides, everyone knows that blindness is a curse from God on those that lead sinful lives. Or on the parents, for the sins they have committed.

2ND PHARISEE: I'm not sure you're right. If this Jesus were a sinner, how could he perform signs like this? *(To the BLIND MAN)* It was your eyes he opened; what do you have to say about him?

BLIND MAN: He is a prophet from God.

1ST PHARISEE: It's no good asking him. Call in his parents! Let's get some answers.

2ND PHARISEE leaves and returns leading the BLIND MAN'S MOTHER and FATHER, who take the remaining stools.

1ST PHARISEE: Is this your son?

MOTHER and FATHER, obviously frightened, nod.

1ST PHARISEE: What kind of a sinful life have you been leading that your son should be so cursed?

2ND PHARISEE: *(To 1ST PHARISEE)* Let's not go into that now. *(To PARENTS)* Do you attest that he was blind from birth?

They nod.

1ST PHARISEE: Then how do you account for the fact that he can see?

FATHER: We know this is our son, and we know he was blind at birth. But how he can see now, or who opened his eyes, we have no idea.

MOTHER: Ask him. He is old enough to speak for himself.

1ST PHARISEE: *(Giving the MOTHER an irritated look and turning to the BLIND MAN)* I insist you give the credit for your healing to God, rather than this . . . this *person*. We know that he is a sinner, so he cannot possibly have been the one who healed you.

BLIND MAN: I wouldn't know if he is a sinner or not. All I know is that I was blind and now I see.

1ST PHARISEE: *(Groaning)* Urrrgh!

MOTHER: *(Innocently)* What's the matter? Aren't you feeling well?

1ST PHARISEE: *(Ignoring her, to the BLIND MAN)* Just exactly what did this man do to you? How did he open your eyes?

BLIND MAN: I have told you once already, but you won't listen. Do you want to hear it all over again? Don't tell me you want to become his disciple, too?

1ST PHARISEE: Certainly not! We are disciples of Moses. We know that God spoke to Moses, but we have no idea where this man comes from. *(Indicating JESUS)*

BLIND MAN: Well, this is interesting! Here is a man who is able to heal blindness and you haven't even taken the trouble to find out where he comes from.

2ND PHARISEE: *(Furiously)* We know he is a sinner and that's enough for us! It was wrong of him to heal you. Blindness is God's curse on you and he is interfering with God's plan. *(To JESUS)* Tell us who you are and what it is you think you are doing here.

JESUS: I came into this world to divide it, to make the sightless *(Indicating the BLIND MAN)* see and the sighted *(Indicating the PHARISEES)* blind.

1ST PHARISEE: You are not counting us in with the blind, are you?

JESUS: If you were truly blind there would be no sin in that. "But we see," you say, and so your sin remains.

1ST PHARISEE: Sinner! Blasphemer! All of you, out! Right now! I won't listen to any more of this nonsense! This cannot be tolerated ... I won't have sinners telling *me* that it's all right to heal the blind! You are blaspheming if you say ...

He pushes them out roughly, continuing to rant at them until he is offstage.

Lent 5
John 11:18-46

1996
6 copies

Raised From The Dead

Cast: JESUS, PETER, MARTHA, LAZARUS

Length: 6 minutes

PETER and JESUS are sitting on their stools. There is an extra stool beside them. MARTHA walks in, carrying hers. She looks very determined.

PETER: Oh, oh, Jesus! Here comes Martha. And she really looks mad!

MARTHA: Lord, my brother Lazarus is dead!

JESUS: Yes, Martha. I know.

MARTHA: I know you know. I sent word to you four days ago to come immediately. Why didn't you come? If you had been here my brother would be alive now.

JESUS: It's still not too late.

MARTHA: Not too late? He's dead. Very dead. Why didn't you come while he was still alive?

JESUS: Martha, do you really believe I could have cured him?

MARTHA: Yes, I do. I believe that you have a very special relationship to the Father, and that whatever you ask of him he will give you. Even now.

JESUS: If you really believe that, why do you think it's too late? Your brother will live again. I am the Resurrection and the Life.

MARTHA: Jesus, please! Don't tease me at a time like this. I've heard you preach before about the Resurrection Day when all the dead will rise. But that's a long time off.

JESUS: No, Martha. That's not what I meant. I'll raise him now, today. Do you believe me?

MARTHA: Well ... of course. If you say so.

JESUS: I have authority over death, given to me by my Father. Do you believe that?

MARTHA: *(Still unconvinced)* I think so.

JESUS: Good! Then let's go to the tomb. *(He gets down from his stool and turns as if to go)*

MARTHA: *(To PETER in a stage whisper)* It's really too bad he got here too late to do anything about Lazarus.

JESUS: *(Turning around)* Martha, what are you saying?

MARTHA: *(Stubbornly)* Well, really, Lord! It's much too late for that. He's been in the tomb for four days. He's decayed by now. *Nobody* has *that* much authority over death. Bringing him back now would break all the laws of nature.

JESUS: *(Getting back onto his stool)* Martha! Trust me! Didn't you hear about Jarius' daughter?

MARTHA: Yes, but that was different.

JESUS: How different?

MARTHA: Well, she hadn't been dead very long, and some people said that perhaps she wasn't dead at all, that perhaps she was only sleeping.

JESUS: Martha! Where is your faith?

MARTHA: It's not that I doubt you, Lord. I believe you could do it.

JESUS: Well, then?

MARTHA: The question is: Do you really want to do it? Perhaps it is your will that he die?

JESUS turns away and puts his head in his hands.

MARTHA: *(To PETER)* He really did love Lazarus! Look how he's crying!

JESUS: *(Pointing to a spot near the stage entrance)* There's the stone to the entrance to the tomb. Martha, remove it!

MARTHA: *(Appalled)* Remove it? Lord! The stench!

PETER: Lord! You don't mean it!

JESUS: Remove it! You said that you believed me. If you believe me, remove it!

MARTHA: I ... I can't.

JESUS: Get Peter to help you. I'm sure you can manage between the two of you.

MARTHA: That's not exactly what I meant. I have an idea! Why don't we just wait until Resurrection Day? It can't be that far off.

JESUS: Do you believe me, Martha?

MARTHA: I ... don't know.

JESUS: Martha. Who do you think I am?

MARTHA: *(In an agony of indecision)* I think ... maybe ... the Son of God?

JESUS: If that's what you believe, then move the stone!

After a mental struggle, MARTHA gets off her stool, motions to PETER, and together they mime rolling a large stone. As they work, JESUS prays.

JESUS: Father, hear my prayer and grant my petition, that these people may learn to have faith in Your power.

LAZARUS: *(Walking out of the tomb. He still has his grave clothes wrapped around him.)* Hi!

MARTHA: He did it! Jesus did it!

JESUS: Thank you, Martha. Didn't I tell you that if you believed in me you would see the Glory of God?

MARTHA: Yes.

JESUS: And what might have happened if you hadn't believed — and hadn't moved the stone?

MARTHA: Do you mean that Lazarus might still be . . . still be in there, dead?

JESUS: He might. Now do you see how important your faith is to me?

MARTHA: My faith, Lord? My faith is important?

JESUS: For those who have faith, God can do anything.

PETER: Really? That's good to know. I, for one, will never doubt you again, Jesus.

JESUS: *(Smiling)* Somehow I doubt that, Peter.

Palm/Passion Sunday
Matthew 26:20-25
Also see Mark 14:17-26; Luke 22:14-23;
John 13:21-31

The Reality Of Evil

Cast: JESUS, PHILIP, JAMES, PETER, JUDAS/SATAN (JUDAS/SATAN may be played by the same person, changing his voice and stance to fit the character, or the voice may be done by a VOICEOVER with JUDAS miming the words.)

Length: 9 minutes

JESUS is sitting with his DISCIPLES.

JESUS: I'm glad we were all able to be together for Passover. I have earnestly desired to eat this meal with you before I go away to suffer.

PETER: Oh, Lord, no! You mustn't say things like that! You won't have to suffer. Not if I can help it!

JESUS: *(Sternly)* Peter! Remember what I've told you! Don't let your own interests get in the way of my Father's plans.

PETER: *(Mumbles)* Sorry, Lord!

JAMES: But Lord, how is this to happen?

JESUS: Truly, I tell you, one of you will betray me to the chief priests and Pharisees.

PHILIP: But, Lord, which of us here would do such a thing? You know us all. You chose us yourself.

PETER: Yes, Lord. And we have come to believe in you and to know that you are the Holy One of God.

JESUS: Yes, I myself chose you twelve. And yet one of you is a devil.

JAMES: Which one is it, Lord? Surely not me.

PETER: It couldn't be me. Is it?

PHILIP: Is it me?

JESUS: The one who has dipped his hand into the bowl with me is the one who will betray me.

JAMES: But we've all done that!

JESUS: He who will betray me knows who it is. The Son of Man must go to His death; so it was written. And the prophecies must be fulfilled. But woe to that one by whom the Son of Man is betrayed. It would have been better for him if he had never been born.

There is a long silence.

JESUS: It is the one for whom I shall dip the morsel and give it to him.

He mimes dipping a piece of bread in some wine and hands it to JUDAS.

JUDAS: Surely it is not I, Rabbi? Is it?

JESUS: *(After a pause)* You have said so yourself.

SATAN enters into JUDAS. During this period the DISCI-PLES freeze at the table as SATAN, speaking through JU-DAS' mouth, converses with JESUS.

SATAN: You're a fool, Jesus!

JESUS: Well, Satan. I see you've finally arrived.

SATAN: I suppose you can tell already that this story isn't going to have a happy ending.

JESUS: That depends on what you mean by "ending."

SATAN: *(Snarls)* This is what I mean by it: Your friends are deserting you and your disciples will soon betray you. Tonight every one of them will lose his faith in you. If you didn't realize that before, it's high time you did.

JESUS: I do realize that.

SATAN: I suppose in the long run it doesn't really matter what these so-called friends of yours do — or don't do. *(Motioning toward the others)* This rabble hardly counts in the greater scheme of things.

JESUS: *(Mildly)* I don't know. I've rather enjoyed associating with this "rabble," as you call them. They're very good company.

SATAN: Yes. I can see that you would. Not something I would care to brag about, however.

JESUS: Simply one more of the differences between us.

SATAN: Tomorrow they'll cart you off to your trial, which you will lose.

JESUS: So I've been told.

SATAN: After that, it's torture, humiliation, and the cross. Not a pleasant way to die.

JESUS: My Father's strength will be sufficient for me.

SATAN: Blast you, Jesus! Does nothing frighten you?

JESUS: Did I say I wasn't frightened?

SATAN: Apparently not frightened enough. If you were, you'd start looking for a way out. *(Pause)* I could offer you that, you know. A way out.

JESUS: I'm sure you could. For a price.

SATAN: The price isn't all that high. Not compared with the benefits you would receive.

JESUS: And those benefits are ...?

SATAN: *(Eagerly)* I was hoping you'd ask. First off, you wouldn't have to die. I know that may not seem like much to a rational spirit such as yourself, but I understand you've become rather attached to this messy mortal world.

JESUS: Yes. I have.

SATAN: *(Shaking his head)* I still can't, for the sake of me, understand why.

JESUS: What else, Satan?

SATAN: Not only would you not have to die, you wouldn't have to suffer. As I described earlier ...

JESUS: *(Impatiently)* Yes, yes! No need to go into detail. I understand completely what is waiting for me.

SATAN: Death wouldn't seem nearly so bad, of course, if you had had a full, rich, productive life to look back on. But it hasn't been quite like that, has it?

JESUS: What do you mean?

SATAN: Well, really, Jesus, what have you accomplished during your time on earth? Do you think your beloved disciples have any clearer understanding of who you are now than they did the day you met?

JESUS turns and gazes at his DISCIPLES but makes no reply.

SATAN: What you have done in your lifetime is negligible by any standards. And now it is finished. Tomorrow you will die — without having accomplished a thing.

JESUS: What do you understand of my purposes, Satan? You have never seen beyond your own self-interest.

SATAN: Still, I could spare you all that.

JESUS: And in return ...?

SATAN: All you would need to do is to acknowledge my superiority. That's not asking too much, is it?

JESUS: Let us argue no longer, Satan. We will never enjoy a true meeting of the minds. Whatever it is you must do now, do it quickly.

SATAN: I will leave you now, but we will meet again. The final test is yet to come. Your strength may not withstand it. One little slip and you will have lost. Then the world will be mine — for all eternity.

JESUS: I've told you, Satan, my strength is not my own, but my Father's in heaven. And that will never fail.

SATAN: *(Sneers)* And if you die, so what? Another life wasted. Nothing more momentous than that.

JESUS: That depends on how you look at it. There is no greater love than this, that a man should lay down his life for his friends.

SATAN: We'll see how you feel about that when you're hanging on the cross.

The DISCIPLES recover from their enforced freeze in time to see JUDAS walking out.

PETER: What was that all about, Lord? Where is Judas going?

JESUS doesn't answer or even seem to hear, but sits staring after JUDAS.

PHILIP: *(To PETER)* Perhaps he sent Judas for more wine. We're running out at an amazing rate.

JAMES: Or to distribute some alms to the poor. After all, he's the one in charge of funds.

JESUS: *(Gazing after JUDAS)* Now is the Son of God glorified, and God is glorified in him. *(Returning to the table)* Let us continue.

PETER: Without Judas?

JESUS: *(Sadly)* Yes. Without Judas. Let not your hearts be troubled nor afraid. I am going to leave you soon, but rather than mourning, you should rejoice. I go to my Father and He is much greater than I.

JAMES: But, Lord! Who will take care of us?

JESUS: I will not leave you desolate. I will come back to you.

PETER: When, Lord?

JESUS: In a little while. And then you will know, without a doubt, that I am in my Father, and you in me and I in you.

PHILIP: But how can you let the evil men do this to you?

JESUS: They are of the devil and hate me without a cause. But the devil, the ruler of this world, has no lasting power over me, for I do as the Father has commanded me. And I do this so that the world may know that I love the Father. Let us pray now.

They all bow their heads.

JESUS: Father, the hour has come. Glorify your Son now, so he may bring glory to you. For you have given me authority over all men to give eternal life to all that you have given to me. And this is eternal life, to know you, the only true God, and him whom you have sent — Jesus Christ.

JUDAS appears, holding a lantern. He comes up to JESUS and kisses him on the cheek.

JUDAS: Hello, Jesus.

JESUS: Hello, Satan.

JUDAS leads the way and JESUS follows him out. The DISCIPLES stare at each other in bewilderment, then follow as well.

Maundy Thursday
1 Corinthians 11:23-32

Unworthy

Cast: Two women, MARGARET and SUSAN, and a
VOICEOVER

Length: 8 minutes

*There are two empty stools center stage. MARGARET and
SUSAN enter quietly and seat themselves on their stools with
bowed heads as if they were in a church pew. After a moment
of silence, we hear the VOICEOVER.*

VOICE: For on the night he was betrayed, Jesus took a loaf
of bread and when he had given thanks, he broke
it and said, "This is my body that is for you. Do
this in remembrance of me." *(Pause)* In the same
way he took the cup also, after supper, saying, "This
cup is the new covenant in my blood. Do this, as
often as you drink it, in remembrance of me." For
as often as you eat this bread and drink the cup, you
proclaim the Lord's death until he comes.

The WOMEN look up and stand as if to go to the altar.

VOICE: Whoever, therefore, eats the bread or drinks the cup
of the Lord in an unworthy manner will be answer-
able for the body and blood of the Lord.

*SUSAN sits down abruptly. MARGARET looks at her ques-
tioningly.*

VOICE: Examine yourselves, and only then eat of the bread and drink of the cup. For all who eat and drink without discerning the body, eat and drink judgment against themselves.

SUSAN remains seated with a stricken look on her face.

MARG: Susan! Aren't you coming to communion?

SUSAN only shakes her head.

MARG: Why not?

SUSAN: *(Miserably)* Oh, Margaret! You wouldn't understand.

MARG: *(Sitting down again)* Tell me. I want to know.

SUSAN: I just don't feel worthy.

MARG: There are none of us worthy. But God has granted us grace.

SUSAN: You heard the scriptures. We must examine ourselves. If we eat and drink without discernment, we call down judgment against ourselves.

MARG: But you have examined yourself, haven't you? And asked forgiveness for your sins?

SUSAN: Well ... Yes.

MARG: So what's the problem?

SUSAN: It's not so much what I've done in the past — I know God has forgiven me. It's what I might do in the future.

MARG: *(Confused)* In the future?

SUSAN: You may not know this, but I did some very bad things in my youth.

MARG: *(Lightly)* Haven't we all!

SUSAN: I mean some *really* bad things. I took drugs, and was promiscuous — *very* promiscuous — and ran away from responsibilities, and let lots of people down. I stole to pay for my drugs, even stole from my parents.

MARG: Well, yes, those things are bad. But you confessed your sins and God has cleansed your heart. *(Pause)* You *did* confess your sins to God, right?

SUSAN: Yes, I did.

MARG: *(Relieved)* Then everything's okay.

SUSAN: *(Firmly)* No. It's *not* okay.

MARG: No?

SUSAN: You see, I can't trust myself anymore. I know what I'm capable of doing — only too well — and I know it would offend God terribly if I did any of those things again.

MARG: *(Slowly)* I suppose it would. But what makes you think you'll ever do those things again?

SUSAN: Because I know how weak I am. And I know how much I liked doing those things. I might go back to that life — at any time.

MARG: *(Shocked)* At any time?

SUSAN: Yes. That's why I have to be so strict with myself. I can't allow myself to do those things ever again. I love God too much now to let that happen. That's why I have to keep myself on a short leash. A very short leash.

MARG: But ...!

SUSAN: Don't try to talk me out of it, Margaret. You're mouthing Satan's words.

MARG: *(Indignant)* I am not!

SUSAN: *(Backing down)* Well, maybe not. But you're trying to make me ... make me ...

MARG: Make you what?

SUSAN: You're trying to make me stop mistrusting myself.

MARG: You *need* to mistrust yourself?

SUSAN: Of course. I'm a sinner. I always have been and I always will be.

MARG: Well, I suppose that could be said for all of us. But, still ...!

SUSAN: Still, nothing. I might do it again. At any moment. And if I do, or if I even think about it, and then take communion ... Well, you heard the scriptures. I will bring judgment against myself.

MARG: Yes, I heard that.

SUSAN: It also says that if we judge ourselves, we will not be judged.

MARG: And what does that mean?

SUSAN: It means if I judge myself, stop myself, God won't have to do it for me.

MARG: So you would rather do it yourself than let God do it.

SUSAN: Absolutely! It would be so humiliating if God had to do it for me. And he might be much ...

MARG: Much what?

SUSAN: Much harder on me than I would.

MARG: I don't know, Susan. I don't think anyone could be harder on you than you are on yourself.

SUSAN: *(Grimly)* God can.

MARG: Is that it? Are you afraid of what God might do?

SUSAN: I know what he has a right to do. I know what his standards are. And I know I have fallen short. Yes, I guess you might say that I'm afraid of him. I'm afraid I will bring his righteous judgment down on my head.

MARG: That's too bad.

SUSAN: But more than that, I'm afraid of myself. I'm afraid I might do something that will lose me God's love.

MARG: It doesn't have to be that way.

SUSAN: Are you saying God *doesn't* bring judgment?

MARG: No. Of course he does. But I'm sure he doesn't want you to be afraid of him all the time.

SUSAN: *(Slowly)* Afraid of him ... and of myself.

MARG: Exactly! God loves you. He doesn't want you to keep beating yourself over the head for your failures.

SUSAN: He doesn't want to punish me? He doesn't want me to pay for what I've done?

MARG: He's already paid for it himself, through the death of his son.

SUSAN: *My* sins?

MARG: Everyone's sins. So now you can relax and enjoy the life he's given you.

SUSAN: Enjoy life?

MARG: Absolutely!

SUSAN: I don't have to keep examining myself for sinful tendencies?

MARG: No more than is necessary.

SUSAN: *(Sighs)* That's a relief!

MARG: Come on! There's still time for communion.

SUSAN: *(Worried)* Do you think I'm ...?

MARGARET gives her a long look.

SUSAN: *(Smiles)* Yes. Of course I am. God's grace has made me worthy.

The two WOMEN get up and walk away as if going to the altar.

A Few Bad Choices

Cast: NARRATOR, JESUS, two DISCIPLES, JUDAS and three SOLDIERS

Length: 10 minutes

NOTE: Due to the scope of the Passion Readings and the fact that those readings are the same for all cycles, these Good Friday skits have been arranged as a series. Cycle "A" covers John 18:1-12, Cycle "B" covers John 18:13-40, and Cycle "C" covers John 19:1-30. Each skit is complete in itself, but the three may be strung together to cover the entire Passion in one presentation. Or they may be spread throughout the service, one skit during each of the Three Hours.

In order to maintain the ease of preparation inherent in Readers' Theatre, there will be only one Reader, the NARRATOR. All other characters will mime the words spoken by the NARRATOR as well as performing the actions that suit those words. With so many scenes and locales to cover in the Passion drama, it would be difficult to restrict the action to seated actors. If the Drama Director wishes, the actors may memorize their parts and speak them themselves.

The NARRATOR is sitting on a stool, alone on the stage.

NARRATOR: Now we come to the last days of Jesus' life. After the heartening events of the previous Sunday, it must have seemed to the disciples as if everything were suddenly going wrong. Just when they thought that Jesus was coming into his own, just when it seemed he might finally attain the grudging recognition of the religious establishment as a legitimate preacher and leader, he began to make what could only seem to those about him as a series of bad choices.

His disciples had watched with growing confidence as Jesus performed many mighty works. And they waited patiently for him to proclaim himself the Messiah of their hopes. During his triumphal entry in Jerusalem, they believed that moment to be at hand.

His enemies, the Pharisees, seemed at a loss. They demanded that he rebuke his followers, but they took no steps of their own to control the joyous frenzy that gripped the city. All that week Jesus remained in the city and people flocked to him. He went to the Temple and turned out the money-changers, with no serious opposition from the priests. Even the Pharisees seemed helpless in the light of his growing popularity.

JESUS walks on stage and stands quietly staring out into the middle-distance. The lights come up on this section of the stage.

NARRATOR: The evening before Passover, Jesus had sponsored the traditional banquet for his closest friends. It was then that they may have had the first inkling that things were not as they should be. His conversation seemed disjointed, a mixture of elaborate plans for the future and intimations of his approaching departure. The disciples were confused. "Lord, where are you going?" they asked. "Why cannot we follow you?" To each other they murmured, "What does he mean by this? We do not understand what he is talking about."

Two DISCIPLES enter and pantomime the words (in quotes) spoken by the NARRATOR. One of the DISCIPLES is carrying a sword.

NARRATOR: They tried to recall him to his higher purpose by asking,

1ST DISCIPLE: *(Pantomiming as NARRATOR speaks)* "Lord, why is it you will reveal yourself to us and not to the world?"

NARRATOR: And to encourage him by stating,

2ND DISCIPLE: *(Pantomiming)* "We know that you know all things and do not need to have anyone question you. By this we believe that you came from God."

NARRATOR: But still Jesus seemed distracted and unmindful of what they considered his true purpose of reclaiming Jerusalem and freeing the people from their political oppressors and false religious leaders. After the meal, Jesus led them into the Garden, there to pray through the night.

While the NARRATOR is speaking, JESUS and the DISCIPLES walk together across the stage. JESUS falls to his knees in prayer. The DISCIPLES first copy him and then slip into attitudes of sleep.

NARRATOR: Whatever the disciples thought of Jesus' request that they pray through the night, they must not have taken it too seriously. They fell asleep in spite of his pleadings to "watch with me." All that changed, of course, with the arrival of a detachment of soldiers and Temple priests led by Judas. The quiet garden was suddenly lit by their torches and the prayerful silence broken by their shouts and

113

demands to see Jesus. The disciples were probably very confused. They had been awakened from a deep sleep and the flickering torches made their surroundings seem unfamiliar and threatening.

JESUS and the DISCIPLES jump to their feet as three SOLDIERS and JUDAS enter. JESUS comes forward to face them.

JESUS: *(Miming the NARRATOR's words)* "Whom are you looking for?"

NARRATOR: They answered:

1ST SOLDIER: *(Miming)* "Jesus of Nazareth."

NARRATOR: Jesus replied:

JESUS: *(Miming)* "I am he."

The SOLDIERS step back once and fall to the ground. JUDAS remains standing.

NARRATOR: Again he asked them:

JESUS: *(Miming)* "Whom are you looking for?"

NARRATOR: And they said:

2ND SOLDIER: *(Miming)* "Jesus of Nazareth."

NARRATOR: Jesus answered:

JESUS: *(Miming)* "I told you that I am he. So if you are looking for me, let these men go." *(Indicating his DISCIPLES)*

NARRATOR: This was to fulfill the word that he had spoken, "I did not lose a single one of those whom you gave me."

The DISCIPLE with the sword steps forward.

NARRATOR: Then Simon Peter, who had a sword, drew it, struck the high priest's slave and cut off his right ear. The slave's name was Malchus.

The DISCIPLE strikes at one of the SOLDIERS.

NARRATOR: Jesus said to Peter:

JESUS: *(Miming)* "Put your sword back in its sheath. Am I not to drink the cup that the Father has given me?"

The SOLDIERS and JUDAS lead JESUS away. The DISCIPLES stand staring after them. As the NARRATOR reads the following passage, the DISCIPLES mime arguing with each other.

NARRATOR: What were the disciples to think? Always before when Jesus had been confronted by hostile crowds or accusations he did not wish to address, he had simply walked away from them, as if he were invincible. Why did he not do that now?

Or, on the other hand, why did he not let his disciples fight for him? Just a few hours before, at the end of the Passover meal, Jesus had spoken to them about the necessity of carrying a sword. Why, then, would he not allow them to use it?

The disciples probably had a pretty clear idea of what an arrest of this sort could mean. It was done in the middle of the night, as are all visits by the secret police. None of the adoring crowds were present to protest his capture; no one would even know what had happened until morning.

Jesus had arranged for his disciples' release, but it was understood they were not to follow him. Why? Even now they might be able to effect a rescue. His most powerful friends, Nicodemus and Joseph of Arimathea, were still ignorant of the situation, but perhaps if the disciples could get to them quickly enough, they could do something to help.

The priests and Pharisees, who just a few hours earlier had seemed virtually helpless in the face of the whole city's approval of Jesus' cause, had turned the tables on them — and Jesus had allowed them to do it. Could he really be as powerful as they had thought?

It seemed a very black day, indeed, for these faithful few. Perhaps the best thing for them to do was to take Jesus' suggestion to heart and make sure of their own skins. And so they ran and kept on running until they were far, far away from the police.

The DISCIPLES turn and leave the stage quickly in the opposite direction JESUS and the others have taken.

NARRATOR: So many of God's actions seem incomprehensible to us, even today. We have our plans for him: he is to be there when we need him to help us overcome our enemies and receive our just reward. But his plans so often seem at odds with ours. The problem is that he is concerned not only with our temporal well-being but with our spiritual growth. If he had done as the disciples wished and put the soldiers to rout, there would have been no crucifixion, no death — and no resurrection. *(Pause)* Let us bow our heads in sorrow that we are not more trusting of the Creator of the Universe. And in gratitude that Jesus does not worry too much about our dissatisfaction with his decisions.

All lights go out for a moment of reflection and then the house lights come up slowly.

Easter Sunday
Acts 10:34-43

As For Me And My Family . . .

Cast: PETER, CORNELIUS, Cornelius' daughter, CLAUDIA

Length: 13 minutes

PETER and CORNELIUS enter and take two of the three stools on stage.

CORN: I'm so glad you could come to visit us, Peter. It's very important for me and my family here present *(indicating the audience)* to learn more about Jesus.

PETER: *(Speaking to the audience)* It's a pleasure to meet all of you. I hope I'll be able to help.

CORN: God made it clear to me in a vision that you were the one we should talk to. One afternoon, at three o'clock, when I was in prayer, he sent an angel to me in a vision. This angel told me that I should send men to Joppa for a certain Simon who is called Peter ...

PETER: That's me.

CORN: ... and that you would be lodging there with a tanner, also called Simon, whose house was by the seaside. As soon as the angel left, I called two of my slaves and a devout soldier from my cohort and sent them to Joppa. You know the rest.

PETER: Yes. And that next day, as your men were travelling to find me, I also had a vision.

CORN: You did?

PETER: Yes, but I didn't understand it at the time. I was on the roof, praying, and became very hungry and wanted something to eat. While it was being prepared, I fell into a trance. I saw the heavens open up and something like a large sheet coming down, being lowered to the ground by its four corners. In it were all kinds of four-footed creatures and reptiles and birds of the air. Then I heard a voice saying, "Get up, Peter, kill and eat."

CORN: But eating creatures like that would be against God's law.

PETER: Exactly! So I said, "By no means, Lord. For I have never eaten anything that is profane or unclean."

CORN: Then what happened?

PETER: The same thing happened twice more. And twice more I refused. Then the sheet was suddenly taken back up into heaven.

CORN: What did all that mean?

PETER: I had no idea. I was very confused. Then your men arrived, and the Spirit spoke to me and told me I should go with them. When your men explained who you were — a Gentile and a Roman centurion — I was even more confused.

118

CORN: Did they explain that I was also a "God-fearer" — one who worships Jehovah as the one, true God and tries to keep the law as best he can?

PETER: Yes. And when I heard that, and realized what it was you wanted — to hear more about Jesus — suddenly I knew what the dream meant: that no longer would it be unlawful for Jews to associate with Gentiles. For God has shown me that I should not call anyone profane or unclean. No longer shall Jews and Gentiles hold themselves apart. The love of Jesus will bring us together to worship God in harmony.

CORN: The Lord has been very good to us. So, now all of us are here in the presence of God to hear what the Lord has commanded you to say.

PETER: *(To the audience)* What I learned from my vision is that God shows no partiality, but in every nation anyone who fears him and does what is right is acceptable to him — Jews and Gentiles, male and female, slave and free. *(To CORNELIUS)* You know about the message he sent to the people of Israel, preaching peace by Jesus Christ — he who is Lord of all. *(To the audience)* That message spread throughout Judea, beginning in Galilee after the baptism that John announced: how God anointed Jesus of Nazareth with the Holy Spirit and with power; how he went about doing good and healing all who were oppressed by the devil, for God was with him.

CORN: Yes, I have heard that message, as have many in my household. And it is wonderful to hear of the wonders that God has wrought. But please go on.

119

CORNELIUS' daughter, CLAUDIA, enters quietly and takes the third stool.

PETER: I am one of the many witnesses to all Jesus did in both Judea and in Jerusalem. They put him to death by hanging him on a tree, just as the prophets foretold, but God raised him on the third day and allowed him to appear, not to all the people, but only to those of us who were chosen by God as witnesses.

CLAUDIA: You were a witness to the miracles of Jesus of Nazareth?

CORN: Excuse me, Peter. This is my daughter, Claudia. She is always eager to learn all she can.

PETER: She is welcome then to ask whatever questions she likes.

CLAUDIA: Thank you.

PETER: Yes, Claudia. I was a witness to all of his ministry. I tell my story to all who will listen.

CORN: How wonderful it must have been to know Jesus personally!

PETER: Yes, it was wonderful. I was also privileged to be one of those chosen to eat and drink with him after he rose from the dead. At that time, he commanded us to preach to the people and to testify that he is the one ordained by God as judge of the living and the dead.

CLAUDIA: But how can you prove that?

CORN: *(Embarrassed)* Claudia!

PETER: No, that's all right, Cornelius. That's a perfectly good question. I'm sure many people will want to know the answer to that.

CLAUDIA: And what is the answer?

PETER: Well, as I said, I was a witness. I saw the miracles with my own eyes. I saw him heal the blind and the lame. I saw him raise Lazarus and Jairus' daughter from the dead. I saw him dead on the cross, and there could be no mistaking the reality of that death. Afterwards, I saw the empty tomb on the third day. I was there when he entered the locked room and showed us his restored body a short time later and after that I ate fish with him on the beach. If anyone knew him, alive and dead, it was me.

CLAUDIA: But what will happen when you're gone? What will happen to your witness then?

PETER: I hadn't thought of that. But I'm sure God has.

CLAUDIA: Is there any other proof?

PETER: Well, there is the fulfillment of the prophecies. All the prophets testify that everyone who believes in him receives forgiveness of sins through his name.

CLAUDIA: That's only of use for those who already believe. What about the rest of us?

CORN: *(Desperately)* Claudia! Don't you have some chores to do — somewhere else?

PETER: That's all right, Cornelius. These are important points she's raising.

CLAUDIA: I've heard the rumors. I've heard that Jesus rose bodily from the dead. But I've also heard it said that his disciples stole the body from the tomb and hid it somewhere to make it look as if he actually did what he said he was going to do.

PETER: Yes, I've heard that rumor, too. *(To the audience)* And maybe many others of you have as well.

CORN: But who would say such a thing?

CLAUDIA: I can understand that, Dad, even if you can't. I've also heard the rumors that Jesus didn't actually die on the cross but only fainted. And that he was taken down still alive.

PETER: *(Impulsively)* But he wasn't alive! I know! I was there! *(Embarrassed)* Well, not exactly. I had run away. But John was. And Mary, his mother, and the other Mary, and Salome. They saw the soldiers stick a lance in his heart and saw the blood pour out. And I helped them carry his body to the burial site. If there had been even the slightest chance that he was still alive, we would have known it. It would have been the best moment of our lives.

CLAUDIA: But what about afterwards? What would you have done if he had lived? He would have been all broken and bloody. And obviously a loser. Nobody would have listened to a thing he said if he hadn't died.

PETER: So?

CLAUDIA: So you would have had to pretend he died and came back from the dead, just for your own sakes.

CORN: *(In pain)* Claudia, is this really necessary?

CLAUDIA: *(Seriously)* It is for me, Dad, if I'm ever to know for sure.

PETER: The trouble is, Claudia, there's no way of knowing for sure. Yes, we could have lied. But we would have all had to lie together. That's harder than it sounds. We were pretty disorganized the days just after his death. The guards were after us and all we could think about was how to get away. We weren't really planning to try to turn the tables on the Temple priests and the Roman occupation, no matter how attractive that might have seemed.

CLAUDIA: But if, as you said, the guards were after you, wouldn't the fact that Jesus was alive have given you some bargaining power?

PETER: You mean, really alive? I don't think so. For one thing, we didn't know it ourselves until Sunday morning. Even then, many of us had a hard time believing it. It wasn't until he came to us in the upper room, that same evening, that we truly believed.

CLAUDIA: That still would have given you plenty of time to cook up a story.

PETER: If we had, I'm sure the first thing the Temple priests would have done is to turn this whole town upside down, looking for the body. It's not that easy to do away with a fresh corpse.

CLAUDIA: *(Suspiciously)* How would you know?

PETER: *(Meekly)* I don't, really. I'm just guessing.

CORN: *(Firmly)* I really don't see how anyone could doubt your word, Peter.

PETER: Well, some day, someone might. So it's better to be prepared. One thing you don't understand, Claudia, is that even now that Jesus is alive, and has been seen by many hundreds of people, it hasn't put us any less in danger from the Temple priests and others of the conservative religious establishment. They're just waiting for a chance to catch us off guard, or outnumbered, and drag us off to prison. So even if we had made this whole thing up, it wouldn't have done us much good.

CLAUDIA: But why would they want to put you in prison?

CORN: I can understand that, Claudia, even if you can't. The message that Jesus preached is pretty radical. It must have upset a large number of people.

CLAUDIA: Who?

CORN: All those with something to lose. All those with a vested interest in the status quo. Rome, for one. The religious establishment, for another. The last thing they needed was some uneducated, wandering preacher telling the people they could speak to God directly instead of through the priests. And have their sins forgiven by Jesus himself instead of offering sacrifice in the Temple.

CLAUDIA: Yeah! I suppose they got a kickback from every sacrifice.

CORN: It's a power thing. No one wants to give up the power they fought for their whole lives, not even to God.

PETER: Especially not to God.

CORN: You're right. That's probably the hardest thing in the world.

PETER: That's exactly the reason people don't want Jesus' resurrection to be true. That's the reason for all these unfounded rumors.

CLAUDIA: What do you mean?

PETER: If it were known to be true, beyond a shadow of a doubt, people wouldn't have any more excuses for not following his teachings, for not worshipping God as Jesus said he wants to be worshipped, from the heart rather than with the mouth. They would have to change their lives, the way they lived, the way they treated other people, the way they thought about money and land and power. It would change everything. And most people don't want that.

CLAUDIA: *(Slowly)* Yes, I can see how that would happen.

PETER: But I know the truth. And so do the rest of the twelve, and hundreds of other people.

CORN: *(Quietly)* I think I'm beginning to know the truth, as well.

CLAUDIA: So what can you do, Peter, to make sure everyone knows? Can you write it down so no one will ever dispute it again?

PETER: I'm just a poor fisherman, Claudia. I can't read *or* write. The only educated ones in our group were Matthew and John.

CLAUDIA: Well someone else, then. Matthew or John. Or someone could take down your words as you said them.

PETER: That would be a good idea. I'll have to think about that. But don't get your hopes up. There's no way to make it foolproof. There will always be people who don't want it to be true. And for them there are no facts on earth that could change their minds.

CLAUDIA: That's pretty pitiful.

PETER: Yes, it is. Frightened people *are* pitiful. But let's remember to pity them instead of hating them for not seeing what we have been given the grace to see.

CLAUDIA: *(Getting down from her stool)* Okay! I feel better now.

PETER: Does this mean I've convinced you?

CLAUDIA: *(Surprised)* Yeah. I guess it does.

CORN: And me as well! So, if no one else has any objections *(Pause, looking to the audience)* I can say with a clear mind, "As for me and my family, we will follow Jesus."

CORNELIUS takes the hands of CLAUDIA and PETER and walks forward to the edge of the stage where they bow to the audience.

Hiding Out

Cast: PETER, ANDREW, SALOME, MARY, mother of James, JESUS

Length: 9 minutes

The four DISCIPLES are seated on stools in the middle of the stage. They look very worried. There is an extra stool near them.

PETER: Andrew, did you lock the doors?

ANDREW: Yes, Peter. I did.

PETER: Are you sure? We can't be too careful, you know.

SALOME: You know the palace guards are looking for us everywhere.

ANDREW: Really, I locked them. And I closed the shutters, too, Salome, so that no one will think there's anyone home. I don't want to be caught any more than you.

MARY: That's good. My son, James, should be here soon. He'll help defend us if anything happens.

SALOME: Don't worry, Mary. Nothing's going to happen.

PETER: How do you know, Salome? How do you know nothing's going to happen? Something very bad could happen quite easily. All it takes is for one person to let spill where we are.

SALOME: *(Indignantly)* I hope you aren't implying that I ...!

MARY: *(Soothingly)* Of course not. No one's accusing anyone. *(Firmly)* Are they, Peter?

PETER: No, no. Especially not you, Salome. But you know as well as I that our ultimate safety depends on staying hidden until the priests and Pharisees give up the search.

ANDREW: I thought everything was going to be so much easier now that Jesus is alive again.

MARY: It's wonderful that he is. It proves he really was who he said he was, the Son of God.

PETER: Yes. It's wonderful. But it doesn't change much as far as we're concerned. It might even make it worse.

ANDREW: Worse? How could it possibly be worse?

PETER: Well, when Jesus was arrested and taken to trial ...

SALOME: Some trial!

PETER: Well, taken before Pilate and the high priests, then, I'm sure the priests and the Pharisees thought they had finally broken the back of our rebellion.

SALOME: Some rebellion!

PETER: Well, that's what they thought it was. And in some ways they were right. Anyway, once they had Jesus they probably thought it would be easy to catch the rest of us and put us to death.

ANDREW: How can it get any worse than that?

PETER: Easy! Now that Jesus has escaped them by rising from the dead, the Temple officials are going to be even madder than before. He's escaped but we haven't, and when they find us they're going to take out all their anger on us.

SALOME: Ouch!

MARY: What can we do about it? How can we protect ourselves?

PETER: I've been thinking about that. For one thing, there's strength in numbers. If we stay close and keep in contact, it will be easier to avoid the soldiers.

MARY: But we can't stay in hiding forever.

PETER: No. I'm sure that sooner or later they'll give up the search. But that still doesn't mean we're home free.

ANDREW: It doesn't?

PETER: No. Even if they let us go back to our homes, we'll still be suspect. They'll be watching us for signs of deviance and lack of cooperation. They'll worry that we might try another rebellion.

MARY: Without Jesus?

SALOME: I don't think so.

ANDREW: Even *with* Jesus I wouldn't want to go through that again.

MARY: How can we convince them we're harmless?

PETER: I'm not sure we ever can. But we can stay out of their way as much as possible.

ANDREW: As you said, there's strength in numbers. What if we were all to, say, move to a remote village? Out of sight, out of mind, as they say.

MARY: That's a good idea! We could live our own life, unbothered by the authorities, and worship in our own way.

SALOME: We could have special schools for our kids and teach them as we think best.

PETER: And if they did come for us there, we'd have a much better chance of defending ourselves.

ANDREW: We might even be able to change the local laws to provide more safety for our people.

MARY: If we're big enough, and strong enough, no one can hurt us — ever again.

SALOME: We might even become a political power in this land.

ANDREW: Yes! And influence the way things are done in Israel. That would be a real witness for our Lord Jesus.

JESUS suddenly appears on stage.

PETER: *(Startled)* Whoa!

MARY: Look! It's Jesus!

ANDREW: Jesus! What are you doing here?

JESUS: *(Taking a stool)* Peace be with you.

MARY: Oh, Jesus! That's exactly what we've been looking for. Peace.

JESUS: And that's exactly why I have come. And why I have risen from the dead — to bring you peace.

PETER: But is it really you?

JESUS: *(Laughs)* Did you think I was a ghost, Peter? No, I'm real. See! Here are the wounds in my hands and my side. Look! The blood has dried but it's real. Believe me.

PETER: *(Looking)* Yes, I do.

MARY: So do we.

SALOME: We believe you, Lord. And we praise the Father for your return.

JESUS: Good! Peace be with you all. As the Father has sent me, so I send you.

PETER: Send us? I didn't know you were going to send us.

ANDREW: *(Suspiciously)* Send us where?

131

MARY: *(Eagerly)* We were thinking of some remote village, someplace quiet ...

SALOME: Someplace where we could live in peace and safety.

ANDREW: And raise our children apart from the wickedness of the modern world.

JESUS: No, I don't think so. I had something a little more rigorous in mind. I had planned for you to go out into the city, two by two, to the highways and the byways, and preach my gospel to the citizens of this wicked world, healing and forgiving sins, doing good to those about you, so that they will come to believe as you do that your Father in heaven wishes only the best for his children.

MARY: But I don't think I could. I'd be too frightened. This city isn't a safe place for women to be. Not to mention the highways and the byways.

ANDREW: Nobody would listen anyway. They're all trying to kill us.

SALOME: What about our children? We can't risk them in some crazy ministry to the poor and downtrodden.

PETER: Jesus, I don't think this is a very good idea.

JESUS: No? Well, just hold still for a moment.

JESUS gets up from his stool and walks down the row, blowing in each person's face in turn and saying, "Receive the Holy Spirit." Then he returns to his stool.

ANDREW: Oh, my goodness! What's happening to me?

SALOME: I feel different.

PETER: I don't feel nearly as afraid.

MARY: Nor do I. I feel like I *could* go out on the highway and tell people about Jesus.

SALOME: I feel like I *could* let my children go to public schools — and deal with the consequences as they arise.

ANDREW: I feel like we aren't as helpless and alone as we thought. *(Turning to JESUS)* It's because you're here.

JESUS: It's because the Spirit's here. The Spirit gives wisdom and courage and other good gifts.

MARY: Praise God for the Holy Spirit. Now we can get out of this stifling room!

SALOME: And rejoin the rest of humanity.

MARY: Is that what you want, Jesus?

JESUS: Yes, it is. It doesn't do to be afraid of people who are not like yourself. They're not monsters of evil, trying to destroy you and your way of life. They are just the same frightened, confused, pitiful creatures you were a few moments ago. And God loves them, every one.

ANDREW: I suppose we should be ashamed.

JESUS: Yes, you should. Self-protection is not one of the qualities I respect. Nor is it one of the gifts of the Spirit. Show the non-believers respect and compassion. Those will take you a lot further than hostility and resentment.

MARY: *(Courageously)* I'm ready for that! Where's the nearest non-believer?

JESUS: *(Pointing)* Right out that door. Go for it, Mary!

MARY gets up and charges out.

JESUS: *(Laughing)* Who's next?

PETER: *(Jumping off his stool)* We all are.

JESUS: Good for you! Now, let's go see what life has in store for us.

They all walk out together, JESUS with his arms around their shoulders.

Reformation Sunday
Jeremiah 31:31-34

Easy Reading

Cast: OTTO and HANS (Gender is not an issue here. If women are used, call them ANNA and GRETA.)

Length: 8 minutes

OTTO and HANS are seated on their stools.

OTTO: Hans, have you heard this new preacher everyone's talking about?

HANS: Which preacher do you mean, Otto?

OTTO: His name is Martin Luther and he's causing quite an uproar.

HANS: No, I can't say I have. What kind of an uproar is he causing, Otto?

OTTO: He's suggesting that we all read the Bible. Each one of us. Individually.

HANS: Boy, that leaves me out. I can't read Latin to save my life.

OTTO: No, Hans. He's translated the Bible into German. He wants us to read it in German, in everyday language.

135

HANS: *(Indignantly)* The Bible shouldn't be written in every-day language. That's a sacrilege!

OTTO: I think it's a good idea, myself.

HANS: You do? But don't you think that's dangerous?

OTTO: Dangerous? How could it be dangerous?

HANS: Well, if we were to read it ourselves, without the guidance of a priest or scholar, we might make a mistake.

OTTO: How could we make a mistake?

HANS: The scriptures are very hard to understand. Their meaning is not always clear. We might think it meant one thing when it meant something completely different. You have to be educated to understand such deep matters. And you know we're not very educated.

OTTO: Martin Luther doesn't think we have to be educated. He thinks the Holy Spirit will guide us.

HANS: That's easy for him to say. He's wonderfully educated and he probably thinks that people like him are the norm. You and I are ordinary people. We wouldn't have a clue what the Bible was talking about.

OTTO: Why don't we give it a try and see?

HANS: *(Appalled)* Give it a try? We can't do that! That would be blasphemy! God wouldn't like it.

OTTO: I don't believe that's true. And neither does Martin Luther.

HANS: Yes, well, where will Martin Luther be when we get blasted by lightning?

OTTO: *(Taking out a Bible)* Come on. Let's try a couple of passages.

HANS: You carry a Bible around with you?

OTTO: Yes. This new translation is so fascinating, I can't put it down. Here, let's take something from the Sermon on the Mount. *(Leafing through)* How about this? *(Reads)* "You are the salt of the earth. But if salt has lost its taste, how can its saltiness be restored?"

They stare at each other for a long moment.

OTTO: Well, that wasn't a good one. Let's try another. How about this? *(Reads)* "You are the light of the world. A city built on a hill cannot be hid. No one after lighting a lamp puts it under the bushel basket, but on the lampstand, and it gives light in all the house. In the same way, let your light shine before others, so that they may see your good works and give glory to your Father in Heaven."

HANS: *(Delighted)* Well, you may be right after all. That certainly seems clear enough.

OTTO: What would you say it meant?

HANS: It's obvious what it means: it means we should do good works and then let the whole world know about them.

OTTO: Well, now, I'm not sure I would agree with you.

HANS: Really? But how can you not? It's so clear.

OTTO: Not at all. Actually, I think it means that inspired by all God has done for us, we share that love by loving others and doing good deeds for them. But we should be sure no one knows it comes from us.

HANS: But that's crazy. It couldn't possibly mean that.

OTTO: Why not?

HANS: Because it very clearly says, "... so that they may see your good works." If you're so modest, how can anyone know what you're doing?

OTTO: Perhaps we're both right.

HANS: We can't both be right. It either means one thing or the other.

OTTO: *(Musing)* But if Martin Luther is right, and the Holy Spirit is truly guiding us, and only one of us can have the correct interpretation, then which one of us is being guided?

HANS: I knew this wouldn't work. We shouldn't even be trying to do this. It's a sacrilege!

OTTO: No, no. Now just calm down a moment. I'm sure there's a logical explanation.

HANS: Logical! The Bible isn't logical. *God* isn't logical.

OTTO: Let's try another one.

HANS: I don't think so.

OTTO: Come on. We've gone this far. We might as well see what we can find. How about this? *(Reads)* "For truly I tell you, until heaven and earth pass away, not one letter, not one stroke of a letter, will pass from the law until all is accomplished."

HANS: Really? It says that? About the law of Moses?

OTTO: Yep!

HANS: But a lot of things that are in the law are no longer observed. What about circumcision?

OTTO: And what about Jubilee?

HANS: What about eating shellfish? This is too confusing.

OTTO: Maybe we aren't doing this right.

HANS: We shouldn't be doing this at all.

OTTO: I know! We should pray to the Holy Spirit for enlightenment. Let's do that now.

They bow their heads in prayer.

OTTO: Okay. Now tell me what those verses mean.

HANS: Well, I think it must be that good deeds are meant to serve as a witness for our faith. I know I have trouble with that. I don't like many people to know I am a Christian. I keep my faith to myself and if I ever do a good deed, I always say it's for tax purposes. Maybe that's wrong.

OTTO: I was just going to say the opposite.

HANS: See! I knew it! I knew we'd never get it right.

OTTO: I'm still not sure there's only one right way. My problem is that I *do* like everyone to see me. I like to brag too much. Maybe it would be better for me to keep quiet and arrange for the glory to go to God and not to me.

HANS: Well ...

OTTO: How about the next one?

HANS: About the law? Well, I think it means that the Old Testament and the New are not really that different. Sure, there may be a few dietary things we don't do nowadays, but basically the teachings about God's mercy and love carry straight on through.

OTTO: I was just going to say —

HANS: *(Interrupting)* I know. Just the opposite.

OTTO: I think that I need to go back to the old scriptures and find new approaches to today's problems. Perhaps some of those old ideas aren't so out-of-date, after all. Take Jubilee. God planned for the lands of the earth to be on loan to us — for our use, but not for our control. We were supposed to return them to the community after we had had the use of them for a certain number of years. Maybe there's a lesson to be learned from that.

HANS: *(Suspiciously)* It sounds as if the Holy Spirit is saying different things to each of us.

OTTO: Yes, it does, doesn't it?

HANS: Maybe that's what divine inspiration is all about.

OTTO: And maybe that's what Martin Luther means when he talks about individual salvation.

HANS: So we no longer need anyone to tell us what the Bible means.

OTTO: " 'No longer shall they teach one another, or say to each other, "Know the Lord." For they shall all know me, from the least of them to the greatest,' says the Lord."

HANS: *(Suspiciously)* Where did you get that?

OTTO: *(Showing the Bible)* In here, where all the answers are.

HANS: Where can I get a copy of that?

OTTO: Come on. I'll show you. *(He gets down from his stool)* You don't think it's wrong then?

HANS: *(Getting down from his stool)* Not while we have the Holy Spirit to make sure we don't go too far astray.

OTTO: I think you're right there!

They leave together.

True Saints

Cast: Two women, NANCY and DEBBY

Length: 6 minutes

The two women are sitting together.

DEBBY: The best thing that ever happened to me was to become a child of God.

NANCY: I feel that way, too.

DEBBY: As a child of God I feel so safe, so loved.

NANCY: I feel that way, too.

DEBBY: I feel that God is watching out for me and that he knows what's best for my life.

NANCY: I feel that way, too.

DEBBY: I feel bubbling over with joy and happiness.

NANCY: I feel ... Well, no. I don't feel that way.

DEBBY: But Nancy! Why not? You should.

NANCY: I guess I don't see the Christian life the same way you do, Debby.

DEBBY: The Christian life is very simple: all we have to do is be like Christ.

NANCY: But what does that mean?

DEBBY: *(Impatiently)* Well, you know! *(More patiently)* Perhaps you don't. Let me explain it to you.

NANCY: Please do.

DEBBY: It's a matter of attitude. If you have a good attitude, you're Christlike. If you don't, you're not.

NANCY: That seems pretty simple. *(Pause)* Perhaps too simple.

DEBBY: What do you mean, "too simple"?

NANCY: Well, how does it work out in everyday life?

DEBBY: It's simple. I mean, it's easy. You know how all the little irritations of life — overdue bills, late buses, running out of gas — seem designed to drive us crazy?

NANCY: Yes.

DEBBY: Well, they are. Or perhaps I should say, "designed to keep us from being Christlike."

NANCY: I can see that. So, how do you cope?

DEBBY: *(Blithely)* I just don't let them bother me, that's all.

NANCY: *(Incredulously)* You don't *let* them?

DEBBY: That's right. I just ignore them. I pretend they're not there. And if people are rude to me, I just smile at them sweetly.

NANCY: I have to say I admire your self-control.

DEBBY: That's what it's all about, isn't it? Behaving as Jesus would have behaved?

NANCY: I'm not sure I could do something like that.

DEBBY: *(Sweetly)* Perhaps some day you will.

NANCY: If I improve sufficiently, do you mean?

DEBBY: Yes. *(Thoughtfully)* Although, I'm not sure everyone can be this Christlike.

NANCY: I think I agree with you there. It would take a saint.

DEBBY: *(Trying to look modest)* It's not all that hard, really.

NANCY: But what do you do when you're angry?

DEBBY: I never get angry.

NANCY: You're kidding!

DEBBY: *(Calmly)* No, anger is not Christlike.

NANCY: What about when you're discouraged?

DEBBY: I never get discouraged.

NANCY: Irritated? Panicked?

DEBBY: Nope! They're not ...

NANCY: *(Sighing)* I know. They're not Christlike. Boy! I can see I've got a long way to go.

145

DEBBY: The important thing is to be nice to everyone. And friendly. And cheerful. Cheerful is very important. Otherwise, you might cause someone else to feel down and then that wouldn't be being Christlike.

NANCY: I can see that. I'm feeling a little down myself right now.

DEBBY: *(Worried)* No, no! You mustn't do that!

NANCY: I'm not sure I know how to stop it.

DEBBY: Prayer! Every morning I spend an hour just asking God to make me friendly and cheerful. And nice.

NANCY: An hour!

DEBBY: *(Frowning)* Of course! You do have a quiet time every morning, don't you?

NANCY: Well ...

DEBBY: If you don't ask, you won't get. James 4:2.

NANCY: But an hour! Just to be nice?

DEBBY: *(Slightly irritated)* That's what it's all about. Being Christlike. There's nothing more important. John 13:35.

NANCY: What are you talking about?

DEBBY: *(Disapproving)* Don't you know your scripture? "By this everyone will know you are my disciples, if you have love for one another."

NANCY: Love is being nice? And friendly? And cheerful? We mustn't forget cheerful — that's the important one.

DEBBY: *(Scolding)* If you're going to mock the Bible, I don't think there's much point in continuing this discussion.

NANCY: I'm sorry. Please go on. I want to know how you do it. I would like to be a saint, too.

DEBBY: *(Slightly mollified)* Well, it's not easy, let me tell you that.

NANCY: No, I imagine it wouldn't be.

DEBBY: You have to hold yourself in at all times. It's a matter of discipline — serious discipline. You can't ever say what you want; you must always say what you should. You have to smile, even if you feel rotten. You have to be cheerful even if you've just heard bad news. You can't have any feelings of your own, only Christ's feelings, which are always good. Emotions can be the death of the Christlike life.

NANCY: Really?

DEBBY: Oh, yes! Once you let emotions in the door, Christlikeness goes right out. You have to watch yourself every minute to make sure you don't let your feelings show.

NANCY: But so often I just don't feel nice.

DEBBY: What does that matter? The Christlike life is not based on feelings, it's based on the will. If you want it to happen, want it strongly enough, it will happen. It's hard, as I said, and perhaps not for everyone. It's taken me years to bring myself under such strict control, but it's worth it, isn't it?

NANCY: I don't know. Is it?

DEBBY: Of course it is! How else can I please God and become a saint?

NANCY: I don't know. But now I understand why there are so few saints.

DEBBY: As I said, It's not for everyone. But come with me now. I have to go to my women's group. You can come along and see how it works out in practice. There will be lots of true saints there — nice women, all friendly, all cheerful.

NANCY: I don't know. I might find it depressing. Such high standards that I know I'll never be able to live up to.

DEBBY: *(Scolding)* Now stop that, Nancy! You can do it if you try. You're just not trying! Now come along and don't dawdle! Don't you want to be like Christ?

NANCY: *(Sighing)* Yes. I do. Okay. I'll come. And I'll try.

DEBBY: Good! I knew you had it in you.

DEBBY and NANCY get down from their stools and go off together.